The last years of BR steam in Wessex:
Western Region

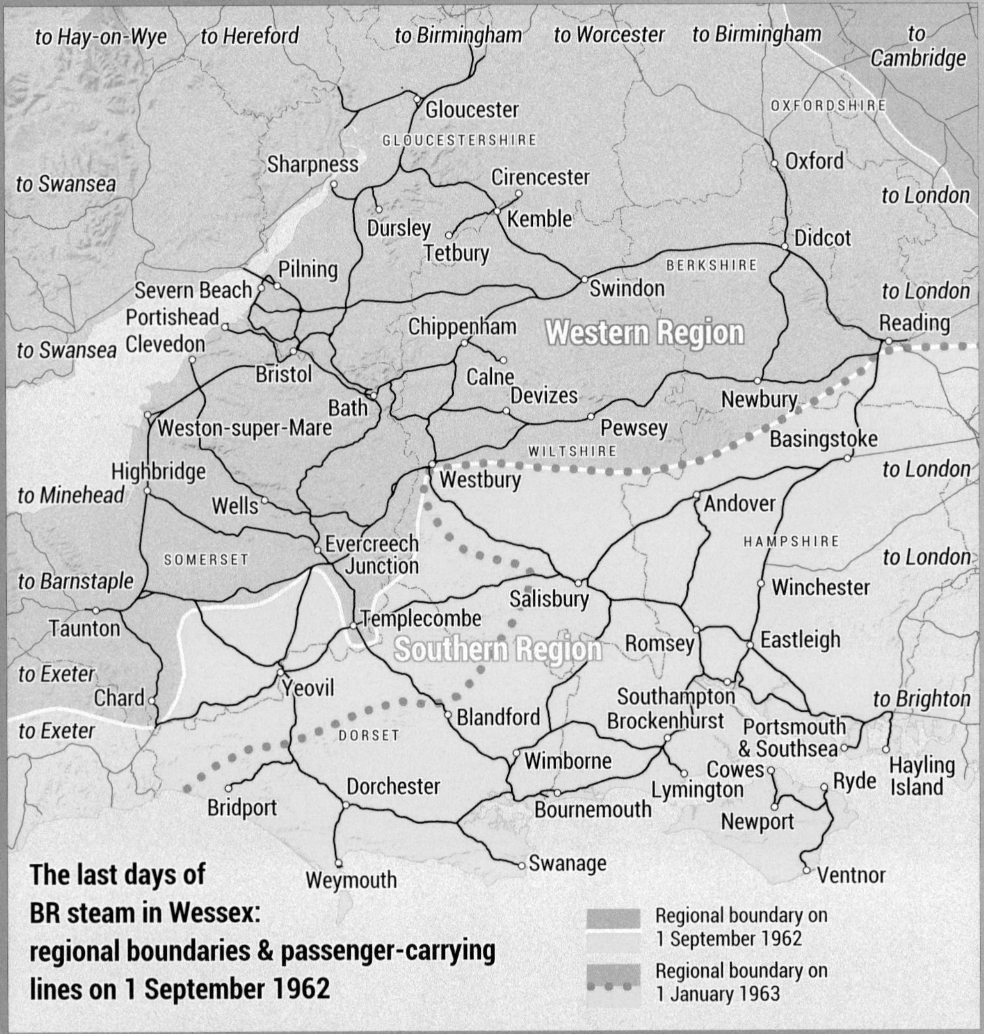

The last days of BR steam in Wessex: regional boundaries & passenger-carrying lines on 1 September 1962

The last years of BR steam in Wessex: Western Region

Philip Horton

SLP

Silver Link Books

First published in 2021

British Library Cataloguing in Publication Data

A catalogue record for this book is available from the British Library.

ISBN 978 1 85794 576 8

Silver Link Books
Mortons Media Group Limited
Media Centre
Morton Way
Horncastle
LN9 6JR
Tel/Fax: 01507 529535

email: sohara@mortons.co.uk
Website: www.nostalgiacollection.com

Printed and bound in the Czech Republic

Contents

Acknowledgements

I would like to thank those who have helped me with my 'Recollections' of 'The last years of BR Steam in Wessex: Western Region'. Many also contributed to my previous publications, including Stephen Edge, who has provided the map, while Ian Bennett has again allowed me to use coloured photographs taken by the late M. E. J. Deane. I must also thank John Price, John Stretton and Neil Carter for allowing me to use some of their photographs. Other photos have come from my own collection, which includes those taken by my late uncle, Denis Horton.

Many of these 'Recollections' are my own but I have also obtained much valuable information from contemporary issues of *The Railway Magazine*, *Trains Illustrated* and *Modern Railways*. Of the many books consulted, Hugh Longworth's *British Railway Steam Locomotives 1948-1968*, published by OPC in 2005, provided the building and scrapping dates for the various steam engines, while the dates of station closures are from *The Directory of Railway Stations* by R. V. J. Butt (Patrick Stephens Ltd, 1995).

The text has benefited from the early proof-reading and editing carried out by my wife Susan. Finally I would like to acknowledge the help and encouragement received from Peter Townsend of Silver Link Publishing and Will Adams of Keyword.

Philip Horton
Lincolnshire
January 2021

Introduction

In my earlier book, *The Last Years of BR Steam around Bath* ('Railways & Recollections' No 64, Silver Link Publishing, 2016), I describe the elimination of steam by diesels in and around the city of my birth. Here I have extended my area of search to cover the whole of 'Wessex', taken as including Somerset, Dorset, Hampshire, Wiltshire, Gloucestershire and Oxfordshire (see the map).

In the following chapters I chronicle the declining use of steam in eight rail centres within Wessex, including their engine sheds and also Swindon Works. The first centre is Bristol, followed by Swindon, Gloucester, Westbury, Taunton, Oxford and Bath (Green Park)/Templecombe. An interlude at an eighth location, Westerleigh, north of Bristol, is covered in Partr 3. The information presented is based on my own recollections and photographs but, as recognised in the Acknowledgements, I have also made use of the notes published in the railway press, while my own photos are ably supported by those of others. Most of these have not been published before.

My own 'trainspotting' days really got under way in September 1959 when I changed schools. I suddenly found myself among many more knowledgeable enthusiasts. Whenever possible a small group of us would set off by train for one of the spotting centres described in the following chapters. In 1964 I managed to acquire a Vespa motor scooter, which increased the opportunities for further visits to these and other rail centres and lineside locations.

Background

Before starting on my account, it is worth giving some background to the situation in which BR(WR) found itself in 1958. After nationalisation, BR's regional boundaries changed several times. Those between the Western (BR(WR)) and Southern BR(SR)), shown on the map, cover the period from 1958 to 1962. In the West Country this closely corresponded with that of the former Southern Railway and GWR. In contrast, the ex-LMS engine sheds at Bristol and Gloucester now came under the control of BR(WR), as did the ex-LMS/S&D sheds at Bath and Templecombe. Even more radical changes came at the end of 1962 when BR(WR) took over all Southern territory west of Wilton, including the engine sheds at Yeovil and Exmouth Junction. These ex-BR(SR) lines are covered in my companion volume, *The Last Years of BR Steam in Wessex: Southern Region*.

The 'Railway Modernisation Plan' of 1955 committed BR to replacing steam traction with diesels, and by 1958 this was being rapidly implemented. At the same time BR(WR) was still improving its fleet of express passenger steam engines by fitting all of its 'Kings' and many 'Castles' with double chimneys and four-row superheaters. In addition the older steam engines were being replaced by BR Standard designs. Swindon works completed the very last of these, 9F 2-10-0 No 92220 *Evening Star*, in March 1960.

The idea of replacing steam with diesels was not a new one. BR had inherited a number of railcars and two experimental AIA-AIA gas-turbine engines from the GWR. In addition BR(WR) possessed seven 0-6-0 diesel-shunters (Nos 15100 to 15106), the first of which had been ordered from English Electric before the war. The similar BR 0-6-0 shunters (numbered from 13000/D3000 (later Class 08)) followed in 1953. As is well known, BR(WR) opted for diesel-hydraulic locomotives to power its main-line trains. The first three designs to appear were the Type 4 AIA-AIA 'Warships' (Nos D600 to D604), the smaller Type 2 B-B units (Nos D6300 to D6357 (Class 22)), both built by the North British Locomotive Co (NBL), and the Type 4 B-B 'Warships' built at Swindon (Nos D800 to D832 (Class 42)) and later at Crewe (Nos D833 to D865 (Class 43)). Both the NBL and Swindon-built 'Warships' appeared in 1958, and the smaller NBL Type 2s a year later, but no further NBL 'Warships' were built. The next to appear were Type 3 B-Bs from Beyer-Peacock (the 'Hymeks', Nos D7000 to D7100 (Class 35)) in May 1961, and the Type 4 C-C (the 'Westerns', Nos D1000 to D1073 (Class 52)). These were also built at Swindon and Crewe, but because of teething problems the first (No D1000 *Western Enterprise*) did not enter service until December 1961.

In autumn 1961 the prototype Co-Co diesel-electric locomotive No D0280 *Falcon* appeared from the Brush Works at Loughborough. After a series of comparative trials at Swindon the diesel-hydraulics were found to be significantly more expensive to run. Their fate was sealed. No more were to be built! The resulting Brush Type 4s (Class 47) started to appear in 1962 and became the standard Type 4 diesel for the whole of BR. A number of English

Electric Type 3 Co-Co diesel-electrics were also built for BR(WR) from 1962 (D67XX (Class 37)). Despite the ban, BR(WR) still managed to build 56 Type 1 0-6-0 diesel-hydraulics at Swindon (the 'Teddy Bears', Nos D9500 to 9555 (Class 14)). By the time they entered service from 1964 their local goods duties had already disappeared under the Beeching Plan, and they were to have a very short life with BR.

The first main-line services to be dieselised were those from Paddington to Plymouth and Penzance. 'Warship' No D800 *Sir Brian Robertson* first hauled the down 'Cornish Riviera' from Paddington on 15 July 1958, closely followed by Nos D600 *Active* and D601 *Ark Royal*, which were used on both the 'Royal Duchy' and 'Cornish Riviera'. Almost a year later, on 16 February 1959, No D800 *Sir Brian Robertson* hauled the 'Bristolian' from Paddington to Bristol for the first time. Dieselisation of the South Wales main line commenced in April 1962 when 'Hymeks' took over the 'Red Dragon' and other expresses. These were replaced early in 1963 by the more powerful 'Westerns', which released the 'Hymeks' to replace steam on trains from Paddington to Worcester and Hereford. The ex-GWR 'North-to-West' route between Hereford and Shrewsbury to Crewe was also an early candidate for dieselisation, together with the ex-LMS line from Bristol (Temple Meads) to Birmingham (New Street). The latter services were still operated by steam engines supplied by BR(LMR), and it was that Region's diesel-electric Type 4 1Co-Co1s, the 'Peaks' (numbered from D11, later Class 45) that were sent as replacements. The first, No D93, arrived in Bristol for crew training in April 1961.

In contrast, the designs of BR(WR)'s DMUs were in line with the rest of BR. 'Cross-Country' units (Class 120), built at Swindon from 1958, soon replaced steam on a number of lines including that between Bristol (Temple Meads) and Weymouth. Among the first local services to receive DMUs (later Class 116) were those around Cardiff and Bristol in January 1958 and May 1959 respectively. Although specific classes of DMU were introduced to each area, including the South West, West Midlands and Thames Valley, they soon moved around the Region. The appearance in 1958 and 1960 of two types of single unit (Classes 122 and 121) saw them replacing steam on many short branch lines. In addition the first of the de luxe Metro-Cammell-built 'Blue Pullmans' started running to Bristol in September 1961, while new 'InterCity' units (Class 123) appeared from Swindon Works in 1963.

While these dates sound quite definitive, the unreliability of these first diesels led to the reappearance of steam on BR(WR)'s expresses into 1964. Steam also reappeared on some summer Saturday trains in 1965. The speed with which steam was replaced was of course greatly helped by the massive closure programme implemented after publication of the 'Beeching Report'. In general it appears that the failure to replace steam with diesel, including on the services from Bath (Green Park), indicated their vulnerability to closure. As it turned out, many of the dieselised services were soon to close too!

Part 1: BRISTOL (Temple Meads)

Train services

In the summer of 1960 Bristol (Temple Meads) was a 'Mecca' for local trainspotters. Not only were there lots of trains, many of which changed engines, but much of the yard of Bristol (Bath Road) shed (82A) was visible from its platforms. Tantalisingly, a boarded crossing led from the platform to the shed, but any spotters trying to cross it were, in my experience anyway, quickly intercepted and ejected.

By 1960 most local trains were worked by DMUs, but there was still a chance of seeing an ex-GWR 'Prairie', Ivatt Class 2 or Standard Class 3 2-6-2 tank. Two of the most anticipated trains were the northbound 'Devonian' from Paignton to Bradford (Forster Square) and later in the day 'The Cornishman' from Penzance to Wolverhampton (Low Level) via Stratford-upon-Avon and Birmingham (Snow Hill). Both trains would arrive at Bristol behind a 'Castle' 4-6-0 but, while 'The Cornishman' would continue behind one of those engines, the BR(WR) engine on 'The Devonian' would be replaced by a 'Jubilee' double-headed with a 'Black 5' or another 'Jubilee' 4-6-0. The two trains also looked different; 'The Devonian' had maroon-liveried coaches, while 'The Cornishman' was comprised of BR Mark 1 coaches in chocolate and cream livery.

At Bristol the up 'Bristolian', comprising a second rake of these latter coaches, would be standing at an adjacent platform. At that time the train ran non-stop to Paddington, since 1959 hauled by a 'Warship' diesel-hydraulic. Apart from a few other 'Warship'-hauled trains and the ubiquitous DMUs, the only other diesels then at Temple Meads were the 0-6-0 shunters, visible from the north-east end of the platforms, which constantly ran in and out of the extensive goods shed.

The line into the docks at Bristol ran next to those to the goods shed. As we discovered one day, it was also possible here to catch a glimpse of one of the two ex-L&Y 0-4-0 saddle tanks, Nos 51217 and 51218 from Barrow Road shed, which shunted the sidings at Avonside Wharf.

BEDMINSTER, BRISTOL: St Philip's Marsh shed's 'Modified Hall' No 7907 *Hart Hall* passes Bedminster, Bristol, with a freight for South West England during the summer of 1963. No 7907, which ended its days at Oxford at the end of December 1965, is also pictured still at work in 1965 (see page 37). *M. E. J. Deane collection, courtesy of Ian Bennett*

After 1960 the replacement of steam by diesels progressed steadily. Among the last to go were the Bristol to Portsmouth trains, which were hauled by ex-GWR 4-6-0s as far as Salisbury until replaced by 'Hymeks' during 1962. In September of that year the destination of 'The 'Cornishman' changed to Sheffield (Midland), and then left Temple Meads behind a 'Peak' diesel-electric heading for Birmingham (New Street). A service that remained steam-hauled into 1963 was that between Yatton and Witham (Friary). The trains were usually in the hands of Bristol-based Standard Class 3 2-6-2 tanks although the last two trains, which ran on Saturday 7 September 1963, were hauled by Class '2251' 0-6-0s Nos 2268 and 3218.

By the summer of 1964 just one steam-hauled passenger train regularly left Bristol for Westbury via Bath, on weekdays. This was the 6.38am from Avonmouth, which called at Stapleton Road and Lawrence Hill in Bristol (see Chapter 5). Another, the 6.10pm from Weston-super-Mare, ran to Swindon on Sundays (see Chapter 2). Both trains were withdrawn at the start of the winter timetable. After that the only regularly steam-hauled trains from Bristol (Temple Meads) were the stopping trains to Gloucester (Eastgate) and Bath (Green Park). The latter included a through train to and from Portishead until that service was withdrawn in September 1964. The Gloucester trains disappeared in January 1965, while those to Bath went at the end of December of that year, the service was withdrawn in March 1966 It was, however, different on summer Saturdays in 1965, when several of the extra trains between the Midlands and the South West were steam-hauled. These included the 8.00am from Wolverhampton (Low Level) to Minehead and Ilfracombe, followed by the 10.05am from Wolverhampton (Low Level) to Paignton. Both trains ran via Stratford-upon-Avon. That summer the extra trains via Birmingham (New Street) were all diesel-hauled, barring failures when steam engines were still substituted.

Left: **BRISTOL (Temple Meads):** A typical view of Bristol (Temple Meads) from Bath Road bridge. 'Hall' No 6932 *Burwarton Hall* of Hereford shed (86C) pulls out of Bristol during the summer of 1960. The train had probably travelled over the North & West route to Bristol via Hereford. The engine ended its days at Oxford at the end of December 1965. *M. E. J. Deane collection, courtesy of Ian Bennett*

Above: **BRISTOL (Temple Meads):** Trains on the main line from Bristol to Birmingham (New Street) were dieselised during the summer and autumn of 1961. The last steam-hauled express on the line that I photographed on 8 March 1965 at Bristol (Temple Meads) was headed by 'Jubilee' 4-6-0 No 45694 *Bellerophon*. The train is thought to be the 6.55am from Derby, on which the 'Jubilee' had presumably replaced a failed 'Peak' diesel-electric. The engine was withdrawn in January 1961.

Bristol (Temple Meads) to Bath Spa

KEYNSHAM & SOMERDALE: During the summer of 1964 only two steam-hauled passenger trains called at Bath Spa. One was the Sundays-only 6.10pm from Weston-super-Mare to Swindon, and the train is seen leaving Keynsham & Somerdale behind Swindon-based 'Modified Hall' No 7926 *Willey Hall* on 5 July. Note the splendid ex-GWR roofed footbridge. No 7926 was withdrawn from Oxford shed in December 1964.

Bristol Sheds

82A

Bristol (Bath Road): closed to steam September 1960

By the autumn of 1960 Bath Road shed was being demolished to make way for a new diesel maintenance depot, and because of its early closure I never visited it in steam days. Prior to demolition it comprised a ten-road straight shed, with two turntables. It was responsible for providing engines for both main-line and local passenger services. Among its allocation of some 90 engines were many ex-GWR passenger and mixed-traffic 4-6-0s and 2-6-0s and 'Large Prairie' and 'Small Prairie' tanks, together with a number of Ivatt Class 2 and Standard Class 3 2-6-2Ts. After closure many of its engines went to St Philip's Marsh shed.

In October 1965, several years after it had reopened as a diesel maintenance depot, it hosted open days where two BR-owned steam engines were exhibited. In 1966 the only BR steam engine was a BR(SR) 'USA' tank, departmental loco No DS234 (formerly No 30064). This engine had been on its way to Meldon Quarry when it was intercepted by BR(WR), which replaced it at the quarry with a diesel shunter! No 30064 is now preserved on the Bluebell Railway.

82B

Bristol (St Philip's Marsh): closed June 1964

Despite its 'B' status St Philip's Marsh was a substantial shed. It comprised two roundhouses, a two-road repair shop and a standard GWR coaling plant. Before the closure of Bath Road its engines were all mixed-traffic, heavy freight or shunting engines. It then received a large number of ex-GWR 4-6-0s. During my visit in June 1962 the shed contained 70 engines, including six 'Castles', two 'Counties', 19 'Halls', five 'Modified Halls' and five 'Granges'. Two Class '47XX' 2-8-0s were also present, together with the shed pilot, 0-6-0 saddle tank No 1365. Among the 'Castles' was the now preserved No 4079 *Pendennis Castle*, which was at its home shed.

When I visited the shed again in March 1963 there were still 47 engines present. These included a row of engines in store alongside the shed building, among them the first of Churchward's Class '47XX' 2-8-0s, No 4700, built at Swindon in 1919. My last visit was at the end of June 1964 when I sadly wandered at will around the empty abandoned buildings. Its remaining steam engines were transferred to Barrow Road shed.

82E

Bristol (Barrow Road) (formerly BR(LMR) 22A): closed December 1965

Traditionally Barrow Road supplied the motive power for trains on the LMS's main line between Bristol (Temple Meads) and Birmingham (New Street). It included one roundhouse and a mechanical coaling plant. In 1958 the shed came under BR(WR)'s Bristol Division, but still retained an allocation of ex-LMS 'Black 5', unrebuilt 'Patriot', and 'Jubilee' 4-6-0s. Its goods engines included ex-LMS 0-6-0s, 8F 2-8-0s and several 'Jinty' 0-6-0 tanks. Ex-GWR Class '2251' 0-6-0s, Class '43XX' 2-6-0s and 0-6-0 pannier tanks were soon added. When I visited the shed in June 1962 it contained 31 engines. These included four 'Jubilees' together with two 'Royal Scots', Nos 46141 *The North Staffordshire Regiment* and 46164 *The Artists' Rifleman*, a class that only appeared regularly at Bristol in 1961 after its displacement by diesels elsewhere. Two of the four preserved 'Jubilees', Nos 45690 *Leander* and 45699 *Galatea*, were Barrow Road engines. Also present were several Standard Class 4 and 5 4-6-0s and two 9F 2-10-0s, but only five of the engines were of GWR origin. The smallest engine on shed that day was the dock shunting 0-4-0 saddle tank No 51218, now preserved on the Keighley & Worth Valley Railway.

By October 1965 the shed's allocation included many ex-GWR 4-6-0s from St Philip's Marsh. Thirty-one engines were again present including a number of Standard Class 3 2-6-2 tanks used on trains to Bath (Green Park), by then the only passenger service where steam was still employed. An engine of note was 'Britannia' 'Pacific' No 70053 *Moray Firth*, a Banbury (2D) engine. The shed also contained several withdrawn engines, including the now preserved 0-6-0 No 43924, together with rebuilt 'West Country' 'Pacific' No 34014 *Budleigh Salterton* and a 'Q1' 0-6-0. The last steam engines stored there came from the former Somerset & Dorset line after it closed in March 1966. These were the last steam engines operated by BR(WR) (see Part 8).

In the days before the diesel-hydraulics a 'Castle' heads a Paddington train towards Bath Spa under Brougham Hayes bridge, Oldfield Park. In the distance pannier tank No 9729 pulls onto the down main line with wagons that it will propel across to the goods yard on the north side of the line. *Denis Horton*

Class '28XX' 2-8-0 No 3866 the last of its Class to be built in December 1942, approaches Brougham Hayes bridge at Oldfield Park with a coal train from South Wales to Southampton during 1960. These trains remained steam-worked into 1965, and No 3866 survived until that July.

Bath Spa

In the summer of 1964 a severe speed restriction was in force just west of Bath Spa station due to roadworks. These involved the replacement of Bath's 'Old Bridge' across the River Avon and included building a second bridge under the main line. Here 'Warship' diesel-hydraulic No D840 *Resistance* is about to leave Bath with the 5.30am Paddington to Plymouth train, which I needed to board very quickly, on 31 August 1964. In the distance a 'Hall' Class 4-6-0 is approaching very slowly with the Mondays-to-Fridays-only 6.40am from Avonmouth to Westbury. This was then the only regular steam-hauled passenger train of the day. Had I boarded the train first I would have obtained a better photo of the 'Hall' from the first coach. Hindsight, eh!

'Castle' Class 4-6-0 No 7024 *Powis Castle* enters Bath Spa with the 6.10pm from Weston-super-Mare to Swindon on Sunday 30 August 1964. The up platform, seen on the left, had recently been extended to avoid trains having to 'pull up'. I enjoyed a spirited run non-stop to Chippenham, but sadly had to leave the train there, returning to Bath behind a 'Western' Class diesel-hydraulic. No 7024 was from Oxley shed, Birmingham, coded 2B by BR(LMR), and was withdrawn in February 1965.

BR(WR)'s 'Farewell to Steam' special approaches Bath Spa on 27 November 1965 behind No 7029 *Clun Castle*. The train was organised to mark the end of steam working on the Region. The engine was subsequently preserved at the Birmingham Railway Museum, Tyseley, and continues to see action on the main line.

In this pre-dieselisation shot, a 'County' 4-6-0 has emerged from Box Tunnel with a down express from Paddington. It will shortly pass Box (Mill Lane) Halt and Box station before arriving in Bath Spa. During the spring of 1964 I saw Swindon-based 'County' No 1011 *County of Chester* at Bath Spa with the very late 1.45pm train from Paddington; it was the last regular steam-worked BR train from Paddington I ever saw.
M. E. J. Deane collection, courtesy of Ian Bennett

Bathampton and Box

Above: Steam still appeared through Bath Spa on trains from the South Coast, which ran via Westbury on summer Saturdays during 1964. Here Standard Class 5 4-6-0 No 73080 *Merlin* comes off the Westbury line at Bathampton with the 9.13am from Bournemouth (Central) to Swansea (High Street) on Saturday 29 August 1964. No 73080 was a Weymouth (70G) engine and was withdrawn in December 1966.

Bristol (Temple Meads) to Weston-super-Mare

A 'Castle' heads the up 'Merchant Venturer' comprising a rake of new chocolate-and-cream-liveried Mark I coaches, from Weston-super-Mare to Paddington past Nailsea & Blackwell. Steam survived a little longer on the 'Merchant Venturer' than on the 'Bristolian' as it was not reported to be diesel-hauled until June 1961. *M. E. J. Deane collection, courtesy of Ian Bennett*

In 1961/62 BR(ER) 'B1' 4-6-0s made occasional forays to Weston-super-Mare with excursion trains from the North. Here No 61153 passes Nailsea & Blackwell with one such train. The 'B1' was built at the Vulcan Foundry, Lancashire, during 1947 and withdrawn in January 1965. *M. E. J. Deane collection, courtesy of Ian Bennett*

Between Bristol and Filton Junction

Left: In 1959 just two stopping trains ran from Swindon to Bristol (Temple Meads) via Badminton, at 7.15am and 5.32pm. These trains were used to 'run in' engines recently outshopped from Swindon Works. Seen at Filton Junction with the afternoon train during that year is the recently restored ex-GWR 'City' 4-4-0, the record-breaking No 3440 *City of Truro*. All stations between Filton Junction and Swindon closed in April 1961 except Badminton, which did so in June 1968. *M. E. J. Deane collection, courtesy of Ian Bennett*

Below: By 1965 BR(WR)'s 4-6-0s were almost entirely restricted to freight working. Here 'Grange' No 6829, of Barrow Road shed, formerly named *Burmington Grange*, is pictured from a passing train heading a coal train from Bristol towards Filton Junction on 8 March 1965. The engine was withdrawn from Worcester shed at the end of November.

Dr Day's Junction, Bristol

Right: 'Black 5' 4-6-0 No 45240 is pictured heading a northbound parcels train past Dr Day's Junction, Bristol, on 23 August 1965. Note the large ex-GWR Dr Day's Junction signal box. The engine survived until April 1967

Left: Class '28XX' 2-8-0 No 3836 of Barrow Road shed runs light engine towards Dr Day's Junction on 23 August 1965. The engine had probably brought a train into Stoke Gifford Yard and is heading for Barrow Road, the only shed still servicing steam in Bristol. At the time it was one of the last of its class still working on BR(WR) and was withdrawn in November 1965.

Branch lines from Bristol

Below: In the early 1950s the original station at Portishead was demolished to make way for a new power station, and a spacious new facility opened in January 1954 together with a new signal box. After this, loaded coal trains ran to the power station from collieries at Radstock. Here, in the early 1960s, a train of empties is seen leaving Portishead behind Class '57XX' and '94XX' 0-6-0 pannier tanks bound for Bath (Green Park). DMUs appeared in 1959 but a handful of trains remained hauled by BR Standard Class 3 2-6-2 tanks and were unadvertised through workings from and to Bath (Green Park). I used one of these trains, the 4.35pm from Portishead, on 12 February 1962. *M. E. J. Deane collection, courtesy of Ian Bennett*

Above: On the Yatton to Wells and Cheddar line, BR Standard Class 3 2-6-2 tank No 82009, then based at Bristol (Bath Road), is seen at Wells (Tucker Street) with a train from Yatton to Witham (Friary) in the summer of 1960. Its last shed was Patricroft depot, Manchester (9H), from where it was withdrawn in October 1966. I travelled on the 6.00pm from Witham (Friary) to Yatton on 28 August 1963 behind Barrow Road-based No 82037, which was withdrawn in September 1965. The passenger service was withdrawn in September 1963. *M. E. J. Deane collection, courtesy of Ian Bennett*

Bristol (Bath Road) shed (82A): closed to steam in September 1960

Above: The westernmost platform ends at Bristol (Temple Meads) gave a mouth-watering view of Bath Road shed. As seen here it contains a large number of ex-GWR 4-6-0s including, nearest to the camera, Bath Road-based No 7034 *Ince Castle*, which was withdrawn from Gloucester (Horton Road) (85B) in August 1965. The tank engines used on local passenger trains were also based at Bath Road, and one of them, an Ivatt 2-6-2, is visible behind the row of 4-6-0s. *M. E. J. Deane collection, courtesy of Ian Bennett*

Right: By 1965 Bath Road depot was devoted to servicing diesels, but at its Open Day on 23 October 1965 two BR(WR) steam engines were displayed. One of them, No 6859, formerly named *Yiewsley Grange*, was in ex-works condition. The engine was shedded at Southall (81G) from where it was withdrawn at the end of November 1965.

The second engine at the Open Day on 23 October 1965 was No 7029 *Clun Castle*. It was also the last working 'Castle' on BR(WR) based on Gloucester (Horton Road). It is pictured again on pages 13 and 40 before it was withdrawn at the end of December 1965.

Bristol (St Philip's Marsh) shed (82B): closed June 1964

Below: Churchward's large Class '47XX' 2-8-0s, first introduced in 1919, still found work on fast freight and the occasional milk and passenger trains into 1963. No 4706 is seen at its home shed, St Philip's Marsh, in 1961. In July of that year it was reported to have taken over the Saturdays-only 7.30am Newcastle (Central) to Paignton train at Bristol (Temple Meads). It later moved to Old Oak Common from where it was withdrawn in February 1964. *M. E. J. Deane collection, courtesy of Ian Bennett*

Below: On 23 June 1962 the shed pilot at St Philip's Marsh was 0-6-0 saddle tank No 1365. The engine, one of five built in 1910, had come from Swindon shed in May 1960 but was withdrawn in December 1962. One of the class, No 1363, is preserved at the Didcot Railway Centre.

Right: No 90516 (ex-WD No 9253) was built at the Vulcan Foundry, Lancashire, in 1945. It was one of 200 engines sold to the LNER, which briefly became that company's Class '07'. When seen at St Philip's Marsh shed on 8 March 1963 the engine was allocated to the former GCR shed at Woodford Halse (2F).

Far right: The first of Churchward's Class '47XX' 2-8-0s, No 4700, was withdrawn from Southall shed (81C) in October 1962, and was stored with other engines at St Philip's Marsh shed for many months. It was pictured there on 1 July 1963.

Bristol (Barrow Road) shed (82E, formerly BR(LMR) 22A): Closed December 1965

Right: There was a good view of the yard at Barrow Road shed from the top of the steps that led down to it from Barrow Road. In this photo from 1961 the yard is still full of ex-LMS engines including 'Jubilees' Nos 45639 *Raleigh* and 45648 *Wemyss*. Also visible are several 4F 0-6-0s, a 'Crab' 2-6-0 and a BR Standard 9F 2-10-0. The two 'Jubilees' were withdrawn in October and February 1963 respectively. To the left of the photographer was the mechanical coaling plant, the destination of the loaded coal wagons seen centre shot.
M. E. J. Deane collection, courtesy of Ian Bennett

Below: After the closure of St Philip's Marsh shed in June 1964 Barrow Road became responsible for servicing ex-GWR engines. One of these, No 7804, formerly named *Baydon Manor*, is seen on 30 May 1965. On 22 April 1964 I had travelled behind this engine, based at Llanelly (87F), from Aberystwyth to Carmarthen. At that time it was already in a filthy state and leaking steam from many orifices. It nevertheless survived until September 1965 when it was withdrawn from Cardiff (East Dock) (then 88A).

Above: After visiting the Open Day at Bath Road depot on 23 October 1965, with a friend I paid a last visit to Barrow Road shed. It contained some 30 engines, about half of which were ex-GWR types. A more traditional occupant was 'Black 5' No 45386. Earlier that month the shed had contained an unusual visitor, Banbury (2D)-based Britannia 'Pacific' No 70053 *Moray Firth*. Among the engines stored at Barrow Road that day were two BR(SR) engines, rebuilt 'West Country' 'Pacific' No 34014 *Budleigh Salterton* and a 'Q1' 0-6-0. No 45386 survived until the end of BR steam in August 1968

Part 2: SWINDON

Train services

My first memory of a visit to Swindon was in the autumn of 1959 when a large group from school set off from Bath Spa in a DMU. Just before Wootton Bassett our DMU was halted by signals and in the distance we soon saw a 'Britannia' 'Pacific' at speed with the up 'Red Dragon' express, which comprised a set of Mark 1 coaches in chocolate and cream livery. We were soon off again and after our train left Wootton Bassett station we prepared for a spotting bonanza as our train passed Swindon Works, outside of which were several dozen steam engines.

Standing on Swindon station today it is hard to imagine the scene in 1960. Then lines seemed to run in all directions, with the Locomotive Works and Carriage Works visible on either side of the main line. A succession of expresses between Bristol or South Wales and Paddington, mostly steam-hauled, roared through the station on its two centre lines while others stopped at the station. In addition, several local passenger services were still steam-hauled, including trains to Bristol (Temple Meads) via Badminton and to Gloucester (Central), but most of the wayside stations on those two lines were to close in April 1961 and November 1964 respectively, although Badminton survived until June 1968. A handful of trains had also run to Swindon Town station on the former Midland & South Western Junction Railway between Cheltenham and Andover until the service was withdrawn in September

The last of the 'Kings' to be withdrawn, from Old Oak Common shed (81A) in December 1962, was No 6018 *King Henry VI*. The engine was not broken up immediately and was used on an SLS Special from Swindon to Birmingham (Snow Hill) on 28 April 1963, seen here before departure from Swindon.
M. E. J. Deane collection, courtesy of Ian Bennett0

Left: No 5098 *Clifford Castle* of Old Oak Common shed stands in the centre road at Swindon station with a parcels train for Paddington on 23 June 1963. At the time 'Castles' still found employment on parcel strains and fitted freights. No 5098 was withdrawn in June 1964.

Right: No 7035 *Ogmore Castle* of Old Oak Common hauls a coal train off the Gloucester line and through Swindon station on 4 April 1964. The engine was withdrawn in June of that year. This was the only steam-hauled train I saw after spending some time at Swindon station.

Swindon shed (82C)

Left: No 6876 *Kingsland Grange* of Pontypool Road shed (86G) stands at Swindon shed in ex-works condition on Sunday 10 November 1963. After a spell at Newport (Ebbw Junction) (86A, later 86B) it moved to Worcester in November 1965, from where it was withdrawn the same month.

1961. There were also a succession of light engines coming off Swindon shed and passing the north side of the station. Some of these reappeared later hauling heavy freights on the station's down through line.

Steam was to steadily disappear, first from passenger trains, then parcels and finally goods. What was possibly the last scheduled steam-hauled passenger train to arrive at Swindon was the 6.10pm from Weston-super-Mare on Sunday 5 September 1964 (see also Chapter 1).

Swindon shed (82C): closed October 1964

Free conducted tours of Swindon Works took place every Wednesday afternoon, starting at the works entrance in London Street. However, visits to the engine shed and scrapyard required a permit, although these were easy to obtain free of charge, especially on Sundays.

Swindon shed (82C) comprised two roundhouses, one of which was reached via the inside five tracks of a nine-road straight shed. When I visited the shed in November 1962 with my school's Model Railway Club the shed contained 39 steam engines. These included two 'Counties', two 'Castles' and several 'Halls', together with two Standard Class 5 4-6-0s. Other engines included Class '2251' 0-6-0s, 'Small Prairies' and 'Large Prairies' and 0-6-0 pannier tanks. Gradually the number there declined, although even in May 1964 a well-maintained 'Castle' was kept in steam in the event of a diesel failure. The shed closed to steam in October 1964.

A number of engines waiting to be broken up were stored in or near to the Works' Stock Shed, which was situated not far from the running shed. Its last occupant was 'King' No 6000 *King George V*, withdrawn in December 1962 and listed for preservation. I had seen it earlier around Swindon Works stored in the open and looking rather the worse for wear. It was later rescued from the Stock Shed by the Bulmer (Cider) family and restored to steam at Hereford in 1971. It is now a static exhibit at Swindon's 'Steam' museum.

Swindon shed closed in October 1964, and on my last visit on 28 February 1965 rather dilapidated BR Standard Class 5 4-6-0 No 73012 was the only tender engine there. Although it had earlier been a Swindon engine, it had been withdrawn from Bristol (Barrow Road) shed in November 1964.

Even during 1964 an engine was kept in steam at Swindon in case of diesel failure. On Sunday 17 May 1964 this role was played by well-turned-out 'Castle' No 7023 *Penrice Castle* The engine was based at Worcester shed (85A), but was transferred to Oxley, from where it was withdrawn in February 1965.

Swindon Works

In the 1960s Swindon Works could be visited without a permit every Wednesday afternoon, when visitors would be taken on a guided tour. My own first visit was on Wednesday 6 January 1960, when I recall seeing the manufacture of almost everything needed to run a railway, ranging from the spoons used in the restaurant cars and station buffets to steam locomotives. The latter was the last of BR's Standard 9F 2-10-0s, No 92220 *Evening Star*, which became the last steam engine built for BR. It left the Works after a naming ceremony in March 1960. Many steam engines were still being overhauled; in the case of the 'Castles' this involved fitting them with double chimneys and four-row superheaters. A long line of 'Warship' diesel-hydraulics were also under construction in the Works, while six-car BR 'Trans-Pennine' units (later Class 124) were being built in the former Carriage Works on the south side of the line.

An engine of a very different vintage was standing alongside the Works building; this was the last of the GWR's 'Dean Goods', No 2516, which was built at Swindon in 1897 and had been withdrawn from Reading Shed (81D) in May 1956. It was later cosmetically restored and exhibited, first in the new Swindon Railway Museum on Faringdon Road and now at Swindon's 'Steam' museum. In contrast, standing nearby was Class '15XX' pannier tank No 1509, built at Swindon in 1949 and withdrawn only ten years later; it was to survive a little longer at the NCB's Coventry Colliery. Sister engine No 1501, later purchased by the Warwickshire Railway Society for use on the Severn Valley Railway, also worked at the colliery. In contrast, during my penultimate visit on Sunday 4 October 1964 I found a few 'Granges' being overhauled together with some Stanier and Ivatt 2-6-0s (just one of the latter remained on my last visit on 28 February 1965). More significant that day was the sight of 'Castle' No 4079 *Pendennis Castle*, now in private ownership, receiving a full overhaul (see Chapter 5). The only engine in steam was the Works shunter, Class '57XX' pannier tank No 3753, which had been officially withdrawn the previous month.

Swindon scrapyard

Unfortunately my early lists of engines from Swindon do not distinguish between the Works and the scrapyard. In 1960 the latter included some fairly ancient types, among them the last Class '2021' pannier tank No 2069 and Class '31XX' 'Large Prairie' No 3103. No 2069 had been built at Wolverhampton in 1899 and was withdrawn in April 1959, while No 3103, built at Swindon in 1907, was withdrawn in January 1960. Over the years the types being cut up became more modern and, during a November 1962 visit, included four 'Kings'. Two, Nos 6023 *King Edward II* and 6024 *King Edward I*, were later sold to Woodhams' Barry scrapyard and were subsequently preserved. An unexpected sight in the scrapyard in October 1965 was 11 ex-LNER 'V2' 2-6-2s, which had come from BR(NER) sheds and had been towed to Swindon for breaking up, as the local yards were fully occupied.

Stored around the Old Gasworks and Stock Shed

Right: No 5815 was the last of 20 Class '58XX' non-push-pull-fitted 0-4-2 tanks built at Swindon during 1931. It is seen stored there on 20 November 1962 and is being 'cabbed' by members of the Kingswood School Model Railway Club. The engine was still there a year later and was not cut up until June 1964.

Top left: Swindon-based 'Hall' No 5943 *Elmdon Hall* is seen stored near the Old Gasworks on 10 November 1963. Although looking in reasonable condition, it had been withdrawn during the previous June.

Left: A year later, on 4 October 1964, 'Small Prairie' No 4569 has taken the place of No 5943. Built in 1924, it had been withdrawn back in July. Two years earlier I had seen the engine in steam at Whitland, a sub-shed of Neyland (87H), in Pembrokeshire.

Above: Parked outside the Stock Shed on 4 October 1964 was one of the last remaining 'Counties', No 1013 *County of Dorset*. The engine had been withdrawn in July together with No 1010 *County of Caernarvon*, both Swindon-based. This left just No 1011 *County of Chester*, another Swindon engine, which was not withdrawn until that November. Behind No 1013 is the ex-GWR dynamometer car.

Outside Swindon Works

Above: Two 'King' Class 4-6-0s, Nos 6025 King *Henry III* and 6026 *King John*, are seen stored at Swindon without their tenders on Sunday 23 June 1963. The engines were withdrawn in December and September 1962 respectively but were retained in case they were needed during the summer season. They weren't!

Above right: The first 'King', No 6000 *King George V*, was withdrawn in December 1962 and, although identified for preservation, doubts were raised about its future. When seen outside the works on 10 November 1963 it looked a sorry sight, stripped of its nameplates and bell. It nevertheless survived and was eventually rescued by the Bulmer (Cider) family in 1968. It was restored to steam but is now a static exhibit at the 'Steam' museum in Swindon.

Right: When visiting Swindon Works on 4 October 1964 I found a number of 'Granges' receiving an overhaul. Two classes of ex-LMS 2-6-0 were also receiving attention, including three Stanier 'Moguls', which had a power rating of 6P5F. One of these, No 42954, was pictured there at around the same time. The engine was withdrawn in February 1967. *Neil Carter*

Above: My last visit to Swindon Works was on 28 February 1965, when only one of the ex-LMS 'Moguls', Ivatt Class 4 No 43003, remained. This was withdrawn in September 1967. Behind is Class '94XX' pannier tank No 9425, built after nationalisation by Robert Stephenson & Hawthorns Ltd in September 1950. It had been officially withdrawn in November 1963.

Above right: The only engine seen in steam on 28 February 1965 was the Works shunter, Class '57XX' 0-6-0 pannier tank No 3753. This engine had officially been withdrawn in January.

Swindon Works scrapyard

Right: By 1964 Swindon scrapyard was busy breaking up the best of the GWR's motive power. Seen through the partly demolished tender of a Collett 4-6-0 on 26 April are the sad remains of 'King' Class 4-6-0 No 6010 *King Charles I*. The engine had been withdrawn in June 1962. To the right, awaiting the cutter's torch, are Class '94XX' pannier tank No 9420 (withdrawn in March), a 'Castle', a Class '57XX' pannier tank and a Class '47XX' 2-8-0. *M. E. J. Deane collection, courtesy of Ian Bennett*

Right: Class '57XX' pannier tank No 9700 is pictured awaiting the cutter's torch in the scrapyard at Swindon on 10 November 1963. The engine was the first of 11 of its class to be fitted with condensing apparatus to work trains to Smithfield Market via the Metropolitan Lines, and all were shedded at Old Oak Common. No 9700 was built by Beyer Peacock in February 1931 and had been withdrawn at the beginning of November. The other 11 were all built at Swindon during 1933.

Left: During the autumn of 1964 surprise arrivals at Swindon for breaking up were several batches of ex-LNER Class 'V2' 2-6-2s. Eleven of the engines are seen here on 4 October, with Nos 60942 and 60809 nearest to the camera. The latter was once named *The Snapper, The East Yorkshire Regiment, the Duke of York's Own*. They had been withdrawn by BR(NER) between May and July 1964.

Part 3: WESTERLEIGH (On the main line from Swindon via Badminton and from Gloucester to Bristol)

Train services

BR(WR)'s South Wales to Paddington main line crossed the ex-LMS line from Birmingham (New Street) and Gloucester (Eastgate) near the village of Westerleigh, north of Bristol. Here a spur between Westerleigh West and Yate South Junctions allowed trains to run from Bristol or South Wales to Gloucester, with another giving access from the Gloucester to Bristol or South Wales lines between Yate South Junction and Westerleigh East Junction. Each main line once had its own marshalling yard, the GWR's at Stoke Gifford and that of the LMS to the south of Westerleigh.

On 31 May 1960 a friend and I cycled to Westerleigh from Bath and installed ourselves in a field from where we would have a view of all passing trains. Sadly my notebook of loco numbers from the period was lost shortly afterwards, but nevertheless I remember some of the trains we saw. Arriving at around 11.00am we were just in time to see the up 'Red Dragon' from Carmarthen to Paddington pass, headed by one of Cardiff Canton shed's 'Britannia' 'Pacifics' with its rake of Mark I coaches in chocolate and cream livery. This was the first of four named trains we saw that day. Two others have already been noted at Bristol (Temple Meads), but each passed Westerleigh using a different route than expected. The first, which passed at around 11.45am on the former LMS route, was the southbound 'Cornishman' behind its 'Castle' Class 4-6-0. Historically the train was making use of the running powers granted by the Midland Railway to the GWR when the line opened in the 1870s, but perhaps hardly relevant in BR days!

The next to appear at about 12.30pm was the northbound 'Pines Express' from Bournemouth West via Bath (Green Park). Its 12 (BR)LMR coaches included portions for Sheffield (Midland), Liverpool (Lime Street) and Manchester (London Road). Most unusually the train was headed by ex-LNER 'B1' 4-6-0 No 61027 *Madoqua*, an engine that would certainly have been a 'cop' if I had not already 'spotted' it on Bath (Green Park) shed the previous evening. The second of the two named trains noted at Bristol (Temple Meads) was the northbound 'Devonian' from Paignton to Bradford (Forster Square). This, as usual, was headed by two 'Jubilee'

On the main line from Swindon via Badminton

Right: In 1960 'Britannia' Class 'Pacifics' were still in charge of expresses from Cardiff to Paddington, including the 'Red Dragon', which roared past us at Westerleigh on 31 May. Here Cardiff Canton-based (88A) No 70016 *Ariel* climbs away from the Severn Tunnel with the 7.50am Fishguard Harbour to Paddington train on 9 May 1958. In September 1961 the 'Pacifics' were all transferred elsewhere to either Carlisle Kingmoor (12A) or Aston (21D) sheds. No 70016 was withdrawn from Kingmoor in August 1967. *Mike Mensing*

4-6-0s and appeared at around 1.00pm. It passed our vantage point on the Paddington line, then used Westerleigh West Junction to reach the Gloucester line at Yate South Junction. Our last named train, before we started our journey back to Bath, was the southbound 'Pines Express' behind its usual 'Black 5'. All trains seen that day were steam-hauled, including local passenger trains between Gloucester (Eastgate) and Bristol (Temple Meads) and from Swindon to Bristol (Temple Meads) via Filton Junction. Many goods trains also passed us, one of which I can remember was hauled by an ex-LMS 4F 0-6-0.

Five years later on 28 June 1965 I returned to Westerleigh, this time on my motor scooter. Although I found the track layout including the signal boxes still in use, as expected all passenger trains were diesel-hauled, while the two local services had been withdrawn. A handful of goods trains proved still to be steam-hauled, all of which are pictured here. The ex-LMS yard at Westerleigh had closed the previous February, so all the trains were heading for, or had come from, Stoke Gifford yard.

I returned on 27 November as a steam-hauled express passenger train, the 'Panda Pullman' from

After the 'Britannias' were transferred away, they were replaced at Cardiff Canton by 'King' Class 4-6-0s. Here, early in 1962, one of the class storms through Patchway with 'The Red Dragon'. The train is comprised of BR Mark I coaches in chocolate and cream livery. 'Hymeks' started to take over these trains from April 1962, but were soon replaced by 'Western' diesel-hydraulics. *M. E. J. Deane collection, courtesy of Ian Bennett*

Paddington to Cardiff and back, was scheduled to pass, hauled by Ian Pegler's ex-LNER 'A3' 'Pacific' No 4472 *Flying Scotsman*. A single goods train, headed by a Stanier 8F, struggled up from Yate South Junction to join the main line at Westerleigh East Junction. Steam haulage on goods traffic to Stoke Gifford yard continued well after the end of steam on BR(WR), and watering facilities were retained there into the summer of 1966. The ex-LMS main line south of Westerleigh was closed in January 1970, although the old marshalling yard later reopened as an oil terminal. All trains to and from the north now run via Bristol Parkway station, with only one of the linking spurs, between Westerleigh East and Yate South Junctions, still in use.

Above right: In 1965 steam on expresses from South Wales to Paddington was a distant memory. On 27 November, however, the late Ian Pegler's ex-LNER 'A3' 'Pacific' No 4472 *Flying Scotsman* was used on the 'Panda Pullman' from Paddington to Cardiff and back. The train, which was run in aid of the World Wildlife Fund, is seen here passing Westerleigh.

On the main line from Gloucester to Bristol

Right: From 1961 'Royal Scot' Class 4-6-0s, displaced from BR(LMR) services elsewhere, started to appear on the Bristol to Birmingham main line. Here No 46132 *The King's Regiment, Liverpool* passes Coaley Junction with a southbound train in the autumn of 1961. The engine was withdrawn in February 1964. *M. E. J. Deane collection, courtesy of Ian Bennett*

Above: BR Standard Class 5 4-6-0 No 73030 speeds south with a special Sunday freight near Wickwar during the spring of 1965. No 73030 was then a Barrow Road engine, but was transferred to Oxford in June from where it was withdrawn that August.

Westerleigh Junction

Above right: Although steam had long disappeared on passenger trains by 1965, it was still well in evidence on freight. The following photos show steam-hauled goods trains I saw during a stay at Westerleigh for much of the day on 28 June. Here Stanier Class 8F No 48632 waits to join the South Wales main line at Westerleigh East Junction with a freight from the Midlands to Stoke Gifford yard. No 48632 was built at Brighton in 1943 and withdrawn in March 1968.

Right: No 48632 was soon followed by another goods train headed by ex-Crosti-boilered 9F 2-10-0 No 92027. The engine is seen heading onto the South Wales main line at Westerleigh East Junction with its train for Stoke Gifford after being held at signals. No 92027 was a long way from home as, at that time, it was shedded at Speke Junction, Liverpool (8C), from where it was withdrawn in August 1967.

Below: The only northbound freight I saw that day was hauled by 'Modified Hall' No 7907 *Hart Hall* (see also page 7). The train is seen approaching the bridge over the former Midland main line, which the train will join at Yate. The engine ended its days at Oxford shed at the end of December 1965. This bridge has now been demolished and all trains use the eastern curve to join the South Wales main line. The former Midland line to Bristol was closed in January 1970 and now ends at the Westerleigh Oil Terminal.

Above: My final southbound goods on 28 June was headed by 9F 2-10-0 No 92209, which is seen here working hard uphill to reach Westerleigh East Junction and Stoke Gifford yard. It was then a Cardiff (East Dock) (88A) engine, but went to Bristol (Barrow Road) that September. It was withdrawn in December 1965. The driver waved to me, indicating that he would like a copy of my photo. I had to visit first Barrow Road, then Bath Road shed in order to discover his name and address. I subsequently sent him this photo and later visited his home in Bristol. The engine was withdrawn from Barrow Road shed in December 1965.

Part 4: GLOUCESTER

Gloucester was among my favourite trainspotting locations as, like Bristol (Temple Meads), both former GWR and LMS engines could be seen. Sitting on the north end of one of Gloucester (Eastgate)'s platforms, it was possible to also observe all the traffic on the line through Gloucester (Central) between South Wales and Paddington and to Cheltenham Spa (St James).

Gloucester (Central) 1964
In the summer of 1964 a number of steam-hauled services still operated out of Gloucester (Central). These included the trains to and from Hereford, usually hauled by an ex-GWR '43XX' Class 'Mogul' or 'Large Prairie' tank. Trains between Cheltenham (St James) and Paddington were also steam-hauled as far as Gloucester. Latterly ex-GWR Class '4575' 'Small Prairies' were among the engines used, and one of them, No 5545, is seen at Gloucester (Horton Road) shed on 10 May 1964. It was one of the last to be withdrawn, in November 1964. *John Price*

Train services from Gloucester (Central)

By 1960 'Cross-Country' DMUs had taken over most of the trains between South Wales and Birmingham (Snow Hill) via Stratford-upon-Avon, but the most prestigious train of the day to use Gloucester (Central) station was still steam-hauled. This was the 'Cheltenham Spa Express' to Paddington, which left Cheltenham (St James) at 8.00am. It reversed at Gloucester, where a 'Castle' would take over for the run to London. During the 1930s the train's predecessor, 'The Cheltenham Flyer', claimed briefly to be the fastest train in the world, at least east of Swindon. Even in 1961, just before the arrival of 'Hymeks', the down train was timed to run non-stop behind a 'Castle' from Paddington to Kemble (91 miles) in 98 minutes. The 'Hymeks' were soon to make their presence felt, although I enjoyed a journey from Gloucester to Stroud behind a 'Hall' as late as February 1963. In contrast, steam survived on trains between Gloucester (Central) and Cheltenham (St James) until December 1965. Meanwhile the heavy freights from South Wales to London or the Midlands were often hauled by Class '28XX' or Stanier 8F 2-8-0s well into 1965 and the latter into 1966.

Far right: Steam remained at work through Gloucester on coal trains from South Wales into 1965 and even 1966. Here 'Manor' No 7811 *Dunley Manor* of Llanelly shed (87F) heads along the centre road at Gloucester (Central) with one of the trains on 31 October 1964. The engine was withdrawn from Cardiff East Dock shed (88A) in July 1965.

Right: Stanier 8F 2-8-0 No 48193 passes through Gloucester with another northbound freight train on 31 August 1965. The train has just passed through Gloucester (Central) station, and the platforms of Gloucester (Eastgate) can be seen to the left. No 48193 was built by NBL in 1942 and withdrawn in January 1968. *John Price*

Over Junction, Gloucester

Left and below left: The last working BR(WR) 'Castle', Gloucester (Horton Road)-based No 7029 *Clun Castle*, comes off the main line from Newport to Gloucester (Central) at Docks Branch Junction with a freight from South Wales on 10 August 1965. The engine was not withdrawn until the end of December 1965 and latterly worked several special trains including BR(WR)'s 'Farewell to Steam Special' in November 1965, as pictured on page 13.

Cheltenham Spa (St James)

Below: BR(SR) 'N' Class 'Mogul' No 31804 is seen at Cheltenham (St James) with the 1.52pm service for Southampton via Swindon (Town) and Andover Junction in the early 1960s. In November 1958 BR(WR) had cut this service to one a day and diverted it from Cheltenham (Lansdown) station, so connections could no longer be made with trains on the Birmingham to Bristol main line. The Andover line closed in September 1961. In the distance an ex-GWR 'Large Prairie' approaches with a train from Gloucester (Central). *M. E. J. Deane collection, courtesy of Ian Bennett*

Another distinctive sight from the end of Eastgate's platforms was of a Class '14XX' 0-4-2 tank propelling its one or two 'auto' or 'push-pull' coaches into the station from Chalford on the Swindon line. Before reaching Gloucester the train would have called at Brimscombe, Stroud and Stonehouse (Burdett Road) stations, together with seven 'Crossing Halts', which had all opened in 1903. On leaving Gloucester (Central), trains for the Swindon line had to cross over the multiple tracks leading into Gloucester (Eastgate) from Cheltenham (Lansdown). After circling around the city the Swindon line joined those from Eastgate to Bristol. The four tracks then ran parallel as far as Standish Junction, where the Swindon line diverged to the east. It was common for trains on the two routes to race each other, including the diminutive 'auto' ones. My first journey on one of the 'auto' trains was on a snowy 11 February 1963 when I travelled from Brimscombe to Gloucester propelled by No 1424. My last was less than two years later, on Saturday 31 October 1964, when I travelled to Stonehouse (Burdett Road) behind No 1458. Despite fierce local opposition the service was to be withdrawn and this was its last day.

By 1965 Gloucester (Horton Road) was home to BR(WR)'s last working 'Castle', No 7029 *Clun Castle*. It was employed on both regular and special trains, including the last scheduled steam-hauled train out of Paddington, the 4.15pm train to Banbury on 11 June and BR(WR)'s 'Farewell to Steam Special' on 27 November 1965 as pictured on page 13. Even after this the engine is reported to have at least twice replaced failed diesels on

Trains from Gloucester (Central) to Chalford

Class '14XX' auto-tank No 1458 stands in Gloucester (Central) station awaiting the arrival of a guard, hauling the delayed 3.08pm to Chalford on Saturday 31 October 1964. The auto-coaches used were built at Swindon in the 1950s. This was the last day of the service; afterwards all wayside stations and halts on the line to Chalford closed, apart from Stonehouse (Burdett Road) and Stroud.

Auto-fitted Class '64XX' pannier tank No 6412 takes water at Stroud before working the 4.40pm train from Stonehouse (Burdett Road) to Brimscombe on 17 October 1964. The engine was active on the last day of the service, Saturday 31 October, and was subsequently preserved, having since worked on several heritage railways. It is now at Buckfastleigh on the South Devon Railway.
John Price

Swindon-based 'Hall' No 5986 *Arbury Hall* stands in Stroud station with a stopping train from Gloucester (Central) to Swindon during June 1961. 'Hymeks' were about to displace steam on these trains. No 5986 was withdrawn from Didcot shed in September 1963. A 'Large Prairie' 2-6-2 tank can be seen taking water in the background. *M. E. J. Deane collection, courtesy of Ian Bennett*

passenger trains; on 11 December it was on banking duties at Brimscombe when it was required to take over the 7.05am Gloucester (Central) to Swindon train. Its last BR run was on 1 January 1966 when it headed the 5.00pm service rom Gloucester to Cheltenham. Horton Road shed then closed to steam and, as is well known, No 7029 was preserved at Tyseley and is currently back on the main line.

Train services from Gloucester (Eastgate)

In the early 1960s the express trains through Eastgate were almost all worked by ex-LMS 4-6-0s. These ranged from a 'Black 5', one of Barrow Road's three unrebuilt Class 6P 'Patriots' or a 'Jubilee' to a 7P 'Royal Scot'. We usually arrived there at 11.19am on board the 10.30am from Bristol to Newcastle, which we had joined at Mangotsfield. If we were lucky the southbound 'Cornishman' from Wolverhampton (Low Level) would still be in the opposite platform behind its 'Castle'. We would then turn our attention to the 11.30am all stations to Birmingham (New Street) via Worcester (Shrub Hill),

Brimscombe

One of the auto-fitted Class '14XX' 0-4-2 tanks is seen leaving Brimscombe with a single auto-coach for Chalford during April 1961. The coach is one of the earlier vehicles that had been converted from a steam railmotor in the 1920s.
A 'Large Prairie' tank can be seen behind the train, stationed at Brimscombe to bank trains up Sapperton bank towards Kemble.
M. E. J. Deane collection, courtesy of Ian Bennett

which would be waiting in the bay platform, usually headed by a 'Black 5'. On one occasion the driver invited us onto the footplate and I realised for the first time the immense size of an engine's firebox! The next named train was the southbound 'Pines Express' at 12.51pm. The northbound train was due at 2.03pm. Prior to that the northbound 'Devonian' had arrived, double-headed from Bristol by two 'Jubilees', one of which was uncoupled to run to Barnwood shed.

Dieselisation of these express services was virtually complete by the start of the winter timetable of 1961, although steam still appeared regularly in place of failed diesels. In the cold winter of 1962/63 steam reappeared, but only to supply heating as the boilers fitted to the 'Peaks' were found to be inadequate. Local trains between Gloucester (Eastgate) and Bristol (Temple Meads) and also Worcester (Shrub Hill) remained steam-hauled until they were both withdrawn from 4 January 1965. During 1964 I managed to travel behind steam on both routes. On 27 May 1964 I caught the 5.25pm from Birmingham (New Street) to Gloucester (Eastgate) at Worcester (Shrub Hill), hauled by 'Black 5' No 44805, and on 31 October 1964 I used the 4.18pm from Gloucester (Eastgate) to Bristol (Temple Meads), headed by Standard Class 4 2-6-0 No 76085, to reach Berkeley Road. Both were Saltley (21A) engines.

As described in Chapter 1, steam still appeared on trains from Wolverhampton (Low Level) to the West Country on summer Saturdays in 1965, but only one, the 6.55am from Wolverhampton (Low Level) to Penzance, called at Gloucester (Eastgate).

St Mary's Crossing Halt
One of the crossing halts opened by the GWR in 1903 was St Mary's Crossing Halt, situated between Brimscombe and Chalford stations. The Halt is pictured in August 1961 with auto-fitted Class '64XX' pannier tank No 6437. The engine, which was withdrawn in July 1963, is about to leave with a train from Gloucester (Central) to Chalford. *M. E. J. Deane collection, courtesy of Ian Bennett*

Chalford

By the summer of 1964 Class '1400' tanks were in short supply and other non-auto-fitted engines had to be substituted. Here 'Large Prairie' No 6106 approaches Chalford's down platform after arrival with the 1.03pm from Gloucester (Central) on 17 September 1964. No 6106 was withdrawn from Southall shed in December 1965 and is now preserved at the Didcot Railway Centre.

Gloucester (Eastgate) 1962

Standard Class 5 4-6-0 No 73021 stands in Gloucester (Eastgate) station with a southbound express on 29 August 1962. To the right, Nottingham (16A)-based 'Black 5' No 44856 stands at the adjacent platform face with a stopping train for Bristol (Temple Meads). At the time No 73021 was a Barrow Road engine, but moved to Gloucester (Barnwood) shed a month later. It was finally withdrawn from Oxford shed in August 1965, while No 44856 lasted until February 1967. *John Stretton*

Left: The last northbound 'Pines Express' was steam-hauled by 'Black 5' No 44659 and is pictured leaving Gloucester (Eastgate) on 8 September 1962. I was waiting at Gloucester to catch the last southbound train to Bournemouth West; it arrived behind a 'Peak' diesel-electric, which was replaced at Bath (Green Park) by 9F 2-10-0 No 92220 *Evening Star*.

Above: Also seen at Gloucester (Eastgate) on 8 September 1962 was one of Barnwood shed's two 0-4-0 dock shunters, No 41535. The engine is making its way from the docks to its home shed. It was withdrawn in October 1964.

After the 'end of steam' at Gloucester

After the official end of BR(WR) steam at Gloucester on 1 January 1966, a remarkable number of steam-worked freights were reported running to or through the city towards Bristol, Swindon or South Wales. BR(LMR)-based 'Black 5s', Stanier 8Fs or Standard 9F 2-10-0s were usually involved, although at least two ex-LNER 'B1s', Nos 61173 and 61199, were also reported. In response, BR(WR) had to provide coal at Horton Road shed. Several Stanier 8Fs reached Swindon, where they had to obtain water and turn in Swindon Works. By 6 June, however, when Stanier 8F No 48747 arrived there with a special freight, the only water facilities were at Kemble. During May two of the class, Nos 48628 and 48254, were employed on engineering trains in connection with work on Sapperton Tunnel. Watering points were also maintained at Stoke Gifford yard and on the South Wales line at Lydney.

Until the beginning of August 1966 it appears that a 'Black 5' had a regular turn on an overnight parcels train from Birmingham (Snow Hill) to Bristol via Stratford-upon-Avon as far as Gloucester. The engine returned on another parcels train to Birmingham (Moor Street) early the next morning. Finally on 13 August No 45493 is reported to have worked into Gloucester with empty pigeon vans. It returned north light engine.

Gloucester (Eastgate) station closed in December 1975, after which trains between Bristol and Birmingham had to reverse in Gloucester (Central) station. Today, however, to avoid this manoeuvre trains pass Gloucester without stopping. Any passengers for Gloucester must change at Cheltenham and get a train in the opposite direction, a total distance of some 15 miles!

Berkeley Road and Sharpness

The stopping trains between Gloucester (Eastgate) and Bristol (Temple Meads) remained largely steam-hauled until January 1965, when they were withdrawn. Here 'Black 5' 4-6-0 No 44663 arrives at Berkeley Road with the 3.45pm train from Bristol (Temple Meads) to Gloucester (Eastgate) on 1 May 1964. This train connected at Berkeley Road with trains to and from Sharpness. On 1 May the southbound connection to Bristol was headed by 'Jubilee' No 45579 *Punjab*. No 44663 lasted until May 1968, No 45579 only until September 1966.

Gloucester (Horton Road) shed (85B): closed December 1965

Horton Road shed in BR(WR)'s Worcester Division included ten roads, split between two straight sheds. I visited it on Sunday 9 September 1962 with the Bristol & District Railway Society and noted 40 steam engines. These included ex-GWR 4-6-0s – six 'Castles', five 'Halls', two 'Modified Halls' and one 'Grange' – together with Class '43XX' 'Mogul' 2-6-0s, Class '2251' 0-6-0s, 'Large Prairie' and 'Small Prairie'
2-6-2Ts, Class '57XX' pannier tanks, a single Class '28XX' 2-8-0, a Class '52XX' 2-8-0T and ex-WD 2-8-0 No 90069. Four Class '14XX' 0-4-2 tanks were present, together with auto-fitted Class '64XX' pannier tank No 6437 (as pictured on page 44). As already mentioned *Clun Castle* was transferred to the shed in October 1964.

Gloucester (Barnwood) shed (85E, formerly BR(LMR) 22B): closed May 1964

Gloucester (Barnwood) shed, which comprised a single roundhouse, was another that I visited several times in the 1960s. Since nationalisation the shed had still been home to some ancient ex-MR engines. These had included 0-6-0 No 58206, which, although subsequently rebuilt, had been constructed by Robert Stephenson in April 1880. It was withdrawn in July 1957. When I visited on Sunday 9 September 1962 I noted 30 steam engines, with ex-LMS 0-6-0s still well represented, including one 'Jinty' tank and both 3F and 4F examples. More modern engines were represented by 4-6-0s from three of the old 'Big Four' companies: ex-GWR 'Hall' No 6940 *Didlington Hall*, ex-LMS 'Jubilee' No 45557 *New Brunswick*, and ex-LNER Class 'B1' No 61083. In addition, the shed contained Standard Class 2 2-6-0 No 78009, several Class 5 4-6-0s and a 9F 2-10-0. On a later visit I found one of the last of ten Derby-built 0-4-0 dock tanks, No 41537, built at Derby. This was withdrawn in October 1963, but a second Gloucester-based engine, No 41535 (as pictured on page 46), lasted until October 1964.

The duties performed by engines from Barnwood shed included a number of ex-LMS branch lines. These included goods traffic to Stroud, Nailsworth and Dursley, and passenger and goods trains between Coaley and Dursley, and from Berkeley Road to Sharpness (the two passenger services were withdrawn from 10 September 1962 and 1 November 1964 respectively). BR(WR) introduced auto-working on the Sharpness line, but the ex-GWR engines involved were still shedded at Barnwood.

When the shed closed its remaining engines, including ex-LMS 0-6-0s, were sent to Horton Road. My last visit to Barnwood was on Christmas Eve 1964, two months after the Chalford 'auto' trains had been withdrawn. Five Class '14XX' tanks were stored there, together with other withdrawn engines including the formerly Redhill-based ex-SR Class 'N' 2-6-0 No 31868.

4F 0-6-0 No 44516 passes Berkeley Road station with a southbound freight on 1 May 1964. No 44516 was withdrawn that September. The Sharpness train, headed by Class '14XX' No 1445 of Barnwood shed, can be seen in the distance.

Gloucester (Horton Road)-based Class '64XX' 0-6-0 pannier tank No 6415 takes water from the ex-Severn & Wye Joint Railway's water tower at Sharpness in August 1961. A year previously the train would have continued over the Severn railway bridge to Lydney; however, part of the bridge was destroyed when, in October 1960, a pair of barges collided with it. Trains then ran only between Berkeley Road on the ex-Midland main line and Sharpness. *M. E. J. Deane collection, courtesy of Ian Bennett*

Above: No 1445 is seen again taking water at Sharpness on 1 May 1964. At 6.00pm it will head the last train of the day back to Berkeley Road. The lady chatting to the driver was the stationmaster. The last day of passenger services was on 31 October when I travelled on this train, hauled by a Class '1453' tank, together with many other enthusiasts.

Above right: Goods traffic from Sharpness continued after the passenger service had been withdrawn. On 28 June 1965 I found 0-6-0 4F No 44269 waiting to leave with a load of timber. The engine was by then based at Gloucester (Horton Road) shed and lasted until the end of BR(WR) steam at the end of December 1965. Until then the nuclear flask trains from Berkeley Power Station were also steam-hauled.

Right: For a time steam engines were broken up at Sharpness by Coopers Metals Ltd. On 1 May the engines there included two Class '43XX' 'Moguls', Nos 6319 and 7335, together with four 'Castles', Nos 4087 *Cardigan Castle*, 5040 *Stokesay Castle* (pictured), 5050 *Earl of St Germans* and 5071 *Spitfire*. all had been withdrawn between August and October 1963

Class '47XX' 2-8-0 No 4701 is seen at Sharpness on 28 June 1965, after the Sharpness scrapyard had gone bankrupt. The remaining engines were sent to Cashmore's yard at Newport for breaking up. In front of No 4701 can be seen the cab of 'Castle' No 7037 *Swindon*; this was the last of its class to be built at Swindon Works in August 1950. After withdrawal in March 1963 there was an appeal to save it for Swindon Town, but this failed to get the necessary support and the engine was broken up.

Part 5: WESTBURY

Train services

Westbury, in Wiltshire, was an important junction and remains so today. It was therefore a candidate for an early trainspotting visit, which a friend and I made in the autumn of 1959. Most of the local trains from Bristol (Temple Meads) through Bath Spa to Westbury were already operated by DMUs, together with those to Weymouth. Trains from Bristol and South Wales to Salisbury and to Portsmouth were, however, still steam-hauled by ex-GWR 4-6-0s. My memories from that visit are of seeing a Standard Class 4 4-6-0 outside the shed, a Class '56XX' 0-6-2 tank on a train of coal empties about to return to South Wales, and the arrival of the down 'Royal Duchy' from Paddington behind (disappointingly) a 'Warship' diesel-hydraulic. The 'Small Prairie' tank that took our train back to Bath was a pleasant surprise.

The arrival of 'Hymeks' during 1962 meant that by the end of that year the Salisbury line trains were also diesel-hauled. Nevertheless, on 12 January 1963 I enjoyed my last run from Salisbury to Bath behind a 'Hall'. Despite the very cold weather, including the heaviest snowfall in two decades, I decided to visit the Hayling Island branch, where I travelled behind 'Terrier' 0-6-0 tank No 32661. I returned on the 4.45pm train from Portsmouth & Southsea headed, as far as Salisbury, by a Standard Class 4 2-6-0. We reached Salisbury in the bitter cold at 7.25pm where the 'Mogul' was quickly uncoupled and disappeared into the murk towards Salisbury shed. I waited for the expected 'Hymek' to appear but nothing happened. Eventually there was a station announcement that our loco had failed; it appeared that 'Hymeks' did not like the cold! The time ticked by and it got colder and colder, until at last the tender of a 'Hall' appeared out of the gloom. It was coupled to our train and we were off to Westbury and Bath. The train soon warmed up and I arrived in Bath without further mishap.

In contrast, Saturday 20 July 1963 was a cloudy, muggy day. My mission was to travel on the line from Chippenham to Westbury. I then planned a journey through Devizes to Patney & Chirton on the West of England main line. This I achieved by catching four different trains, all worked by DMUs. Despite that, I had several interesting encounters with steam en route. While at Chippenham I spotted 'Castle' No 7029 *Clun Castle*, then an Old Oak Common engine, leaving the station on time with the 9.45am service to Weston-super-Mare. It was the last 'Castle' I ever saw on a scheduled Paddington to Bristol train.

Ex-GWR 'Hall' Class 4-6-0 No 6955 *Lydcott Hall* stands in Westbury station after arrival on the 6.38am all stations service from Avonmouth via Bristol (Stapleton Road) on 12 February 1964. At the time this was the last steam-hauled passenger train on the route. I had travelled on the train from Oldfield Park. The engine was withdr.awn later that month..

Arriving at Trowbridge I had some time to wait for my train to Devizes. While I was there several summer Saturdays-only trains passed through or called at the station; these included trains from Bournemouth (Central) to Cardiff, Swansea (High Street) and Nottingham. Until September 1962 the latter train would have run via Bath (Green Park). Shortly before I left Trowbridge for Devizes, the Weymouth to Wolverhampton (Low Level) arrived at around 1.05pm. My notebook shows that while at Trowbridge I saw Nos 6940 *Didlington Hall* and 6941 *Fillongley Hall*, and No 5039 *Rhuddlan Castle*, but does not record which trains they were working. The South Wales trains also ran during 1964 usually headed by BR(SR) Standard Class 5s, which included Nos 73080 *Merlin* and 73082 *Camelot*. A year later, on 7 August 1965, I saw No 6838 *Goodmoor Grange* leaving Weymouth with its train to Wolverhampton (Low Level).

After a change of DMU at Devizes I eventually

arrived at Patney & Chirton on the West of England main line. Here I also had a long wait and was able to observe the passing trains. Although the expresses were all in the hands of 'Warships', a steam-hauled goods train passed through the station in each direction. The first clanked slowly through on the down line behind Southall-based Class '47XX' 2-8-0 No 4707. I discovered that the train was being stopped because of a hot box on one of the wagons. This was eventually shunted into a siding on the down side of the station and detached. Soon after the station closed in April 1966 the signal box was demolished and the siding taken up. In contrast, the second, an up goods, was also headed by a Swindon-built 2-8-0: Stanier 8F No 48412. This came roaring through the station on the long climb to the line's summit at Grafton. Although I had hoped that the 4.07pm from Reading to Trowbridge via Devizes would be hauled by a Westbury 'Hall', it eventually arrived behind a 'Hymek'!

Two passenger trains through Bath Spa to Westbury remained steam-hauled into 1964, and both called at Oldfield Park. The first was the early-morning 6.38am (Saturdays excepted) from Avonmouth Dock via Bristol (Stapleton Road), while in the early evening the 7.00pm came from Bristol (Temple Meads). The latter disappeared at the start of the 1964 summer timetable, but the Avonmouth

Steam specials through Westbury in 1965 and 1966

On 9 May 1964 'Castle' No 4079 *Pendennis Castle* famously failed with melted firebars while working Ian Allan's high-speed special from Paddington to Plymouth. No 4079 was subsequently purchased privately and restored at Swindon Works. To celebrate its resurrection, on 2 October 1965 Ian Allan organised the 'Pendennis Castle Special' from Paddington to Plymouth, with No 4079 working to Exeter (St David's) and back. The train is seen here during a water stop at Westbury.

LNER-designed 'A2' 'Pacific' No 60532 *Blue Peter* is seen at Westbury on 14 August 1966. The engine had just come off the LCGB's 'A2 Commemorative Railtour' and was declared a failure. The railtour had left Waterloo in the morning and was to return via Exeter (Central), Exeter (St David's), Taunton, Westbury and Salisbury. Several other specials to Exeter had overcome BR(WR)'s steam ban during 1966.

train survived until the end of that summer. I travelled on it on 12 February 1964 when I arrived at Westbury behind No 6955 *Lydcott Hall* as pictured on page 52.

My next three arrivals at Westbury were all steam-hauled specials. The first, on 2 October 1965, was Ian Allan's 'Pendennis Castle Special', which celebrated No 4079's return to the main line. The engine had suffered a disastrous failure while passing Lavington when working Ian Allan's 'Castle' high-speed special from Paddington to Plymouth on 9 May 1964; the train was commemorating GWR 4-4-0 *City of Truro*'s epic run down Wellington Bank on 9 May 1904, together with the end of steam on BR(WR) generally. The story of *Pendennis Castle*'s rescue by 'Modified Hall' No 6999 *Capel Dewi Hall* and the outstanding performances of the three other 'Castles' involved has recently been told by Gary Boyd-Hope in the May 2020 edition of *The Railway Magazine*. As noted in Part 2, in February 1965 *Pendennis Castle*, by then in private ownership, had been undergoing a major overhaul at Swindon Works, and worked its special from Paddington to Exeter (St David's) and back without mishap. After a spell in Australia the engine is now back at the Didcot Railway Centre and should soon be back in steam.

My next railtour was the LCGB's 'A2 Commemorative Railtour' behind LNER-designed No 60532 was to be replaced at Westbury on the LCGB's 'A2 Commemorative Railtour' by 'Britannia' 'Pacific' No 70004, once named *William Shakespeare*, from Crewe South shed (8B). Now running very late, No 70004 heads the train at Westbury and, although due to be replaced at Salisbury by No 60532, in the event hauled the train through to Waterloo.

The last BR operated steam-hauled passenger train to run down the WR's West of England main line from Reading to Exeter (St David's) was the Southern Counties Touring Society's 'West Country Special' on 13 November 1966. Here Standard Class 5 4-6-0 No 73065 has arrived at Westbury after hauling the train from Victoria. The engine is about to be replaced by unrebuilt 'West Country' 'Pacific' No 34019 *Bideford*.

Class 'A2' 'Pacific' No 60532 *Blue Peter* on 14 August 1966. The train had started at Waterloo and ran to Westbury via Exeter (Central) and Exeter (St David's). By the time the train arrived it was running very late and the 'A2' was taken off and declared a failure. Fortunately 'Britannia' 'Pacific' No 70004, once named *William Shakespeare*, was waiting to take the train on to Salisbury, where, after servicing, the 'A2' should have resumed the journey back to Waterloo. In the event the 'Brit' worked our train through to its destination.

My last railtour was the Southern Counties Touring Society's 'West Country Special' on 13 November 1966. This was the last BR steam-hauled passenger train to run down the West of England main line from Reading to Exeter (St David's). At Westbury Standard Class 5 4-6-0 No 73065, which had brought the train from Victoria, was exchanged for unrebuilt 'West Country' 'Pacific' No 34019 *Bideford*. The train ran to Exeter (St David's) before continuing to Yeovil Junction via Exeter (Central). At Yeovil the 'West Country' was replaced by a 'Merchant Navy' 'Pacific'.

Westbury was to see active steam into 1967 as BR(SR) engines still arrived on special goods trains from Weymouth. Although steam on the Region officially ended on Saturday 8 July 1967, Weymouth shed (71G) turned out Standard Class 5 No 73092 to work a perishables train as far as Westbury on Sunday the 9th.

Westbury

Above right: No 34019 *Bideford* backs on to the 'West Country Special'. The engine hauled the train via Exeter to Yeovil Junction, where it was replaced by a 'Merchant Navy' 'Pacific'.

Dilton Marsh Halt, Westbury-Salisbury line

After discovering No 5988 *Bostock Hall* inside Westbury shed being coaled up to work a special freight to Salisbury on 9 July, I made my way to Dilton Marsh Halt to await its passing. After what seemed like hours I was about to leave when I heard the train coming, working up the grade towards Warminster. I just had time to get this shot of it passing above a graveyard below the halt. The engine was withdrawn from Tyseley shed (BR(LMR) 2A) that October.

Westbury shed (82D, later 83C): closed September 1965

Westbury shed was a typical 'Churchward'-era GWR shed with four straight roads and a turntable situated to the south of and behind the shed building. I made several visits to it, including on 8 March 1963 when I recorded 24 engines. By then its former allocation of 'Small Prairie' and Class '54XX' 0-6-0 pannier tanks had disappeared. The two 2-6-2 tanks present were 'Large Prairie' No 4174 and 'Ivatt' Class 2 No 41208. Ten 'Halls' were noted, including the first of the 'Modified Halls', No 6959 *Peatling Hall*. A year later 47 engines were on shed, but many were stored awaiting their turn at the breaker's yard. On my final visit, on 11 July 1965, I found ten engines in more or less working condition, including No 5988 *Bostock Hall*, which was being coaled up to work a special goods train to Salisbury, and No 6803 *Buckleby Grange*. In addition, two Class '57XX' pannier tanks were in light steam under the coal stage, while five others were in the shed building.

While I was waiting for *Bostock Hall* on the platform of Dilton Marsh Halt, '28XX' Class 2-8-0 No 3844 drifted downhill light engine towards Westbury. This engine was withdrawn from Bristol (Barrow Road) shed in October 1965.

Westbury to Patney & Chirton via Devizes

Devizes once had a frequent train service that included through trains between Paddington and Bristol, but these disappeared in the winter timetable of 1961/62, after which DMUS became dominant. Steam lasted longer on the local pick-up goods and, although usually worked by one of Westbury's pannier tanks, in the summer of 1961 Westbury-based 'Small Prairie' No 4567 was pictured at Devizes with one of the trains. The engine was withdrawn in September 1962. *M. E. J. Deane collection, courtesy of Ian Bennett*

Above: On Saturday 20 July 1963 I arrived at Patney & Chirton station on the West of England main line from Trowbridge, following a change of DMU at Devizes. My hope was that the 4.07pm from Reading to Trowbridge via Devizes, one of the last through trains on this route, would be hauled by a Westbury 'Hall'. In this I was disappointed, as it eventually arrived behind a 'Hymek'. I did, however, see two steam-hauled freight trains. The first arrived behind Southall-based Class '47XX' 2-8-0 No 4707, and was stopped to detach a wagon on which a hot box had been detected. The second, an up goods, was headed by another Swindon-built 2-8-0, Stanier 8F No 48412. The station closed in April 1966 together with the Devizes branch.

Westbury shed (82D, later 83C)

Above right: The first 'Modified Hall', built at Swindon in March 1944, No 6959 *Peatling Hall*, is seen in light steam on Westbury shed on 8 March 1963. At that time the engine was based at Old Oak Common, and was withdrawn from Oxford shed at the end of December 1965.

Right: For a time Westbury shed was used to store engines before their journeys to the breaker's yard. On 1 March 1964 Class '2251' 0-6-0 No 2200 was among those stored at its home shed. Although the first of its class numerically, it was not built at Swindon until June 1938, while the first of the class was No 2251, built there in March 1930. No 2200 had been withdrawn in September 1962.

Also in store at Westbury on 1 March 1964 that day was 'Small Prairie' No 5544, which had once been a Truro engine (83F). It had also been withdrawn in September 1962

When I visited Westbury shed on 11 July 1965 I was surprised to find that it still contained active steam. Here Class '57XX' pannier tanks Nos 4607 and 9605 are pictured under the coaling stage. Both engines lasted until September 1965, when Westbury shed closed.

Part 6: TAUNTON

Train services

Taunton's position on the main line from Paddington to Bristol (Temple Meads) and the South West made it a busy place for trainspotters, particularly on summer Saturdays. Its expresses were dieselised by the end of 1961, although on summer Saturdays 'Kings' and other ex-GWR 4-6-0s still appeared on the holiday trains until September 1962. I remember arriving at Taunton from Bath Spa in April 1961 behind a 'Castle' on the 7.30am from Paddington to Paignton, then still a scheduled steam turn. Before arriving at Taunton the train passed the wayside station at Durston, where the line from Yeovil came in on our left; it then crossed above the main line from Westbury before running parallel to it from Cogload Junction into Taunton. At the start of 1962 Taunton was still the starting point for several steam-worked services. These included the stopping trains to Westbury, Bristol, Exeter (St David's), Barnstaple Junction, Minehead, Yeovil (Pen Mill) and Chard (Central). The stopping trains to Westbury and Chard were withdrawn that September.

In the summer of 1963 when I visited Taunton again the Bristol trains were diesel-worked, as were the local trains to Minehead. Some of the summer through trains to Minehead were, however, still steam-hauled, as were the stopping trains to Exeter (St David's), while Class '43XX' 'Moguls' were in use on Barnstaple Junction trains. The only other steam-worked line into 'Wessex' was that to Yeovil (Pen Mill), on which the trains were usually hauled by either an ex-GWR 'Large Prairie' or 'Small Prairie' or a Standard Class 3 2-6-2 tank. My first journey over the line was on 28 August 1963 when I caught the 12.58pm from Taunton to Yeovil (Pen Mill) behind Taunton based 'Large Prairie' No 4143. This train ran along the West of England main line as far as Langport, thereby missing out the short section of branch line from Durston.

As I wanted to travel on this part of the line, hopefully behind a 'Small Prairie', I travelled to Yeovil on 12 February 1964, aiming to catch the 11.21am from Pen Mill. I was in luck as the train was headed by Yeovil Town (83E)-based Class '4575' 'Small Prairie' No 4593. After calling at Langport (West) our train ran along the West of England main line but soon turned off to the right to reach Durston, a typical Brunel-designed ex-Bristol & Exeter Railway station. After leaving the station our engine had to work hard to lift its train over the flyover at Cogload Junction. Steam was then turned off as the train dropped down to run parallel with the West of England main line, calling at Creech St Michael Halt before arrival in the rain at Taunton. The engine was destined to haul the last passenger train to Yeovil on 13 June; en route it passed 'Large Prairie' tank No 4131 heading in the opposite direction.

Left: During the summer of 1963 a number of other branch and local passenger trains were worked by steam engines from Taunton shed, including those to Barnstaple (Junction). On summer Saturdays there was a train each way between Wolverhampton (Low Level) and Ilfracombe, which also included through coaches to and from Minehead. Here Taunton resident Class '43XX' 'Mogul' No 6363 has arrived from Barnstaple as a 'Warship' approaches the station on an up express.
M. E. J. Deane collection, courtesy of Ian Bennett

Below left: Class '47XX' 2-8-0s continued to see occasional use on passenger trains into the summer of 1963. Here Old Oak Common-based No 4704 stands in Taunton station with a westbound passenger train during the summer of 1962. During the previous July the engine was reported to have hauled the Saturdays-only 1.20pm from Paddington to Kingswear. It was withdrawn in May 1964.
M. E. J. Deane collection, courtesy of Ian Bennett

Below: Another Class '43XX' 'Mogul', No 6326, is seen arriving at Taunton with the 8.35am from Barnstaple on 31 August 1964. Later that day I enjoyed a trip to Barnstaple (Junction) behind No 6363. The trains remained steam-hauled until Taunton shed closed in October 1964 when both 'Moguls' were withdrawn. Trains to Barnstaple were then worked by DMUs until the service was withdrawn from 3 October 1966.

Taunton shed (83B): closed October 1964

Taunton shed always seemed to be rather run down with its single gloomy roundhouse. It was nevertheless a 'B' shed in BR(WR)'s Newton Abbot Division and once had an allocation of almost 70 engines. I visited the shed twice in 1963 and once, for a final time, in February 1964, following my journey behind 'Small Prairie' No 4593. My 1964 visit actually produced the greatest number of engines (45), including Reading-based 'Castle' No 5076 *Gladiator* and three 'Halls', one of which was St Philip's Marsh's 'Modified Hall' No 7909 *Heveningham Hall*. One of the 'Halls', No 4989 *Cherwell Hall*, and two Class '28XX' 2-8-0s, Nos 2822 and 2827, were Taunton-based engines, as were the four Class '57XX' 0-6-0 pannier tanks and seven Class '43XX' 'Moguls'. Two of the latter, Nos 7322 and 7326, had been built in 1932 with cab windows. Only one 'Small Prairie', No 5548 (of Yeovil (Town) shed), was present, together with four BR Standard Class 3 'Prairie' tanks. Three of these, Nos 82001, 82030 and 82044, survived until December 1965, ending their days on trains between Bristol (Temple Meads) and Bath (Green Park) (see Part 8). Two auto-fitted Class '14XX' 0-4-2 tanks, Nos 1442 and 1466, had only recently arrived at Taunton, together with No 1450, following the closure of Exeter (St David's) shed (83C) in October 1963; they worked the 'auto-trains' between Tiverton and Tiverton Junction until the service finished in November 1963. No 1466 was withdrawn that December and is now preserved at the Didcot Railway Centre. Nos 1442 and 1450 survived until May 1965 working auto-trains between Yeovil (Town) and Junction and, in February 1965, on the Seaton branch. Both engines were subsequently preserved, No 1442 in Tiverton Museum and No 1450 presently on the Severn Valley Railway.

Taunton-Highbridge line

At Highbridge the ex-GWR's Bristol to Taunton main line crossed the ex-S&D's line to Burnham-on-Sea. Looking north, the Burnham line can be seen between the signal box and the road overbridge. In the distance a 'Hall' approaches with a westbound express during 1961. The station buildings were designed for the Bristol & Exeter Railway by Brunel, but have since been flattened. *M. E. J. Deane collection, courtesy of Ian Bennett*

Class '57XX' No 9670 leaves the ex-GWR goods yard at Highbridge with the afternoon pick-up goods to Taunton on 8 March 1963. This would have been a nice photo had not the signal post been in the way! Taunton-based No 9670 was withdrawn in June 1965. (For pictures of Highbridge S&D, see Part 8.)

Taunton-Yeovil (Pen Mill) branch

Above: Another service from Taunton that remained largely steam-worked in 1963/64 was that to Yeovil (Pen Mill). Here Taunton-based 'Small Prairie' No 5521 stands at Langport (West) with a train from Yeovil to Taunton in the early 1960s. No 5521 was withdrawn in April 1962 but after a spell in Barry scrapyard was rescued and is now based on the South Devon Railway at Buckfastleigh.
M. E. J. Deane collection, courtesy of Ian Bennett

Centre: My first journey from Taunton to Yeovil was on 28 August 1963, when I caught the 12.58pm from Taunton, headed by Taunton's 'Large Prairie' No 4143. The train is seen at Yeovil (Town) station before departing along the single line to Yeovil (Pen Mill). The engine was later transferred to Radyr shed (88B) in Cardiff, from where it was withdrawn in June 1964.

Right: My final journey from Yeovil to Taunton was on 12 February 1964. As I had hoped, my train, the 11.21am from Pen Mill via Durston, was hauled by Class 4575 'Small Prairie' tank No 4593. The engine is seen in the rain after arrival at Taunton. No 4593 was to haul the last passenger train to Yeovil on 13 June and was withdrawn that September.

Taunton shed (83B): closed October 1964

Above: By 1964 Taunton was the last shed in the Newton Abbot Division to still have an allocation of Class '43XX' 'Moguls' and Class '45XX' 'Small Prairie' tanks. The three 'Moguls' shown here all appear to be in store, while nearer the camera is a Class '28XX' 2-8-0, which is in steam. 'Hymek' No D7023 is to its rear. Behind the engines is the shed's corrugated-iron repair shop. The date is probably 1964. *M. E. J. Deane collection, courtesy of Ian Bennett*

Part 7: OXFORD

Train services

In the early 1960s Oxford station was another magnet for trainspotters. Lines radiated out from it in all directions, the most important of which were the ex-GWR main lines from Paddington to both Worcester/Hereford and Birmingham (Snow Hill) via Banbury. In addition, the ex-LMS cross-country route to Bletchley and Cambridge brought in engines of both LMS and LNER origin. Finally it also saw through trains between the South Coast, the West Midlands and the North East. As a result it was one of the few stations on BR to see engines from all of the pre-nationalisation 'Big Four' railway companies.

As steam was run down, Oxford became the place to see ex-GWR 4-6-0s on Class 1 passenger duties. During the summer of 1963 the Paddington to Worcester trains were the last to be 100% steam-worked, by Worcester (85A)-based 'Castles'. Their duties included the 'Cathedrals Express', which, like most of the Paddington trains, started from Hereford and changed engines at Worcester (Shrub Hill). BR(WR) then announced with some fanfare that the 'Castles' would be replaced by 'Hymeks' at the start of the winter timetable of 1963/64. Nevertheless, on 18 October I went to Oxford in the hope that, following a diesel failure, a 'Castle' might still appear on one of the trains which I would then travel on to Worcester. I had a permit for the shed and asked the shedmaster if there were still steam workings between Oxford and Worcester.

In 1960 Worcester shed (85A) still had a stud of 1940s-built 'Castles' for its Paddington trains. One of them, No 7002 *Devizes Castle*, is seen at Oxford with the 'Cathedrals Express' from Paddington to Worcester and Hereford during 1960. No 7002 was withdrawn from Worcester shed in March 1964. *M. E. J. Deane collection, courtesy of Ian Bennett*

On 18 October 1963, a full month after 'Hymeks' had officially taken over the Paddington to Worcester trains, 'Castle' No 7034 *Ince Castle* appeared on the 11.13am from Paddington to Worcester (Shrub Hill) and Hereford. Soon afterwards No 7005 *Sir Edward Elgar* arrived with the 11.10pm from Worcester (Shrub Hill) (10.05am from Hereford) to Paddington. I then enjoyed a spirited run behind No 7005 to Reading (General). This engine was withdrawn in September 1964, while No 7034 lasted until June 1965, based at Gloucester (Horton Road).

He assured me there weren't, so I returned to the station to catch the next train to Reading, where I planned to do some more shed bashing.

My train was the 10.05am from Hereford and Worcester to Paddington, which, fortunately as it turned out, was running late. Before it arrived I was able to see the arrival of the 11.15am from Paddington to Worcester and Hereford headed by No 7034 *Ince Castle*. When my own train arrived it too was steam-hauled by No 7005 *Sir Edward Elgar* (built as *Lamphey Castle* in 1946 but renamed to commemorate the centenary of Elgar's birth in 1957). After departure from Oxford it ran non-stop to Reading, keeping up a cracking pace and recovering several minutes en route.

I did achieve my ambition of travelling to Worcester behind a 'Castle' on 27 March 1965 on board an Ian Allan railtour from Paddington to Nottingham (!) headed by No 7029 *Clun Castle*. At the beginning of 1964 the 'Cathedrals Express' reverted to steam haulage to road-test several surviving 'Castles' to identify the best for Ian Allan's high-speed special from Paddington to Plymouth on 9 May (see Chapter 5). As mentioned in Chapter 4 a BR(WR) 'Castle' made a last appearance at Oxford when *Clun Castle* worked the last scheduled steam-hauled train out of Paddington, the 4.15pm train to Banbury, on 11 June 1965.

Later that year Oxford was providing another

Top right: Stopping trains between Oxford and Banbury were steam-hauled until withdrawn from 2 November 1964. Here 'Large Prairie' No 4154 stands in Oxford station with the 5.25pm to Banbury on 27 June 1964. The engine was among the last of its class when withdrawn in October 1965.

Below: On 25 November 1965 the 10.10am Poole to York train arrived at Oxford behind Standard Class 5 4-6-0 No 73114, once named *Etarre*. Here No 6872 *Crawley Grange*, lacking both number and nameplates, has taken over the train as far as Banbury. A Brush Type 4 diesel-electric (Class 47) would then take the train on to York.

Right: In November 1965 steam was still well in evidence at Oxford on both passenger and goods trains. Class '57XX' pannier tank No 3677 is seen passing through Oxford station with a transfer goods on the 25th. The engine was among the last of its class on BR(WR) to be withdrawn, at the end of December.

opportunity to travel behind an ex-GWR 4-6-0 on Class 1 passenger work. The train involved was the daily (except Sundays) through train from Newcastle (York from 6 September) to Poole. This ran via the former Great Central Railway line through Woodford Halse to Banbury, then Oxford. Beyond Oxford it called at Reading (West) and Basingstoke, where it joined the BR(SR) main line to Southampton and Bournemouth. At this time the 'Pines Express' was also steam-hauled between Bournemouth and Oxford, usually by a Bulleid 'Pacific'.

On 20 October 1965 I travelled by motor scooter to Reading (West) to catch the northbound York train, which arrived behind BR Standard Class 5 4-6-0 No 73114 *Etarre*. This gave me a good run to Oxford, where it was replaced by No 6872 *Crawley Grange*, lacking both name and number plates, to take the train on to Banbury, where the 'Grange' would have been replaced by a diesel-electric. While waiting at Oxford for the arrival of the southbound York train there was still a smattering of steam to enjoy on freight and trip workings, while at 2.04pm the 'Pines Express' left for Bournemouth behind 'Battle of Britain' 'Pacific' No 34090 *Sir Eustace Missenden, Southern Railway*. My train, the 10.08am from York, soon appeared behind a very tired-looking 'Hall', No 6952 *Kimberley Hall*, which also lacked its name and number plates. It nevertheless gave me a spirited run to Reading, where I left the train to continue its journey to Bournemouth.

Train services into 1966

Steam was officially eliminated from BR(WR) lines from the beginning of January 1966. On Monday 3 January, to mark the end of steam, Oxford shed turned out now preserved 'Modified Hall' No 6998 *Burton Agnes Hall* to haul the Poole to York train as

Above: Rebuilt 'Battle of Britain' 'Pacific' No 34090 *Sir Eustace Missenden, Southern Railway* stands at Oxford station with the southbound 'Pines Express' from Manchester (Piccadilly)/Liverpool (Lime Street) to Poole on 20 November 1965. The 'Pacific' had replaced a Brush Type 4 diesel-electric (Class 47).

Above right: Banbury-based No 6952, once named *Kimberley Hall*, waits to leave Oxford with the 10.08 York to Poole through train on 20 November 1965. I travelled on the train as far as Reading (West). These were the last Class 1 duties performed by ex-GWR 4-6-0s on BR(WR), and Oxford was among the last sheds to service BR(WR) locos. It closed at the end of December 1965.

Between Oxford and Reading

Right: On Saturday 30 January 1965 I travelled to Tilehurst to photograph Sir Winston Churchill's funeral train. While waiting, rebuilt 'West Country' 'Pacific' No 34047 *Callington* passed me with the southbound 'Pines Express'. By coincidence, the following Monday I saw *Callington* leave Bath (Green Park) with the 4.20pm to Bournemouth West.

far as Banbury. As at Gloucester, the proximity of BR(LMR) steam meant its occasional appearance at Oxford until the middle of the year. In addition, although the 'Pines Express' was now dieselised, the Poole to Newcastle trains were still steam-hauled through Oxford.

On 24 June 1966 my destination by motor scooter was the ex-GCR station at Rugby (Central). Here I caught the southbound train, headed by Type 4 diesel-electric No D1773 (later Class 47 No 47178/47588) as far as Banbury, where 'Black 5' No 44710, instead of an ex-GWR 4-6-0, was waiting to take the train on to Poole. In due course the northbound train arrived behind 'West Country' 'Pacific' No 34012 *Launceston*, which was replaced by No D1773. As we left the station *Launceston* was taking much needed water in the bay platform. No facilities for steam were provided by BR(WR) between Basingstoke and what was now BR(LMR) at Banbury.

Oxford shed (81F): closed December 1965

Oxford shed was a sprawling affair that included a four-road straight shed with a coaling stage and turntable situated to the west. For those without a permit a good view of part of the shed yard could be obtained from the towpath of the adjacent River Isis. A list of the engines visible on 8 October 1961 included three 'foreign' engines: ex-LMS Class 7F 0-8-0 No 49425 from Nuneaton shed (2B), a Fairburn Class 4 2-6-4 tank, and ex-LNER 'K3' 2-6-0 No 61801 from Cambridge Shed (31A). On 24 June 1962, when I visited with the Bristol & District Railway Society, I noted 38 engines. These included five 'Castles', five 'Halls' and one 'Modified Hall'. Also present were three Class '14XX' 0-4-2 tanks, Nos 1440, 1442 and 1450, which were soon to be displaced by DMUs on the Abingdon branch. Each found work elsewhere, No 1440 at Gloucester (Horton Road), the other two at Exeter (St David's). 'Foreign' engines included BR(LMR) Standard Class 4 4-6-0 No 75051 of Bletchley shed (1E), 9F 2-10-0 No 92052 of Annesley shed (16B) and BR(SR) Class 'U' 2-6-0 No 31808 of Eastleigh shed (71A).

Oxford shed maintained a fleet of 'Halls' and 'Granges' to the very end of BR(WR) steam. It will be noted from the photo captions that many of the engines featured ended their days at Oxford in December 1965.

Left: 'Battle of Britain' 'Pacific' No 34051 *Winston Churchill* passes Tilehurst with the former Prime Minister's funeral train. The 'Pacific' hauled the train from Waterloo to Hanborough for Blenheim Palace, on the line from Oxford to Worcester. His funeral cortège then travelled by road to St Martin's Church, Bladon, for the burial. No 34051 is now part of the National Collection and is displayed at 'Locomotion', Durham.

Below: 'Modified Hall' No 6999 *Capel Dewi Hall* of Oxford shed is pictured near Pangbourne in the Thames Valley on 20 November 1965. It is heading a goods train for the West Midlands, which I saw again later that day at Oxford. The 'Hall' had its day of fame when it took over Ian Allan's high-speed special from the failed *Pendennis Castle* at Lavington and hauled the train to Taunton (see Chapter 5). The engine lasted until the end of steam in December 1965.

Oxford shed (81F)

Above: Oxford shed was renowned for the variety of engines that it usually contained. Although these were predominantly of GWR origin, engines of the other three pre-nationalisation railway companies could be seen, together with BR Standard engines. Present there on 24 June 1962 was Didcot-based (81F) Class '2251' 0-6-0 No 2221, which survived until November 1964. Among the 'foreign' engines that day was ex-SR Class 'U' 'Mogul' No 31808 of Eastleigh shed (71A).

Right: Among the home-based engines at Oxford on that same day was auto-fitted Class '14XX' 0-4-2 tank No 1442, together with Nos 1444 and 1450. They were soon replaced by DMUs on the branch from Radley to Abingdon. Thereafter both engines went to the West Country and became the last of their class to see active service on the Seaton branch in February 1965. Both were subsequently preserved, No 1442 in Tiverton Museum while No 1450 is now based on the Severn Valley Railway. No 1444 went to Gloucester (Horton Road) and was withdrawn in October 1964.

Last scheduled steam-hauled trains over BR(WR): Reading (West) to Banbury

Right: At the end of 1962 Banbury shed had come under the control of BR(LMR), changing from 84C to 2D. However, it continued to have a stud of ex-GWR engines, which were gradually replaced by ex-LMS types. Defying the WR(BR) ban on steam, 'Black 5' No 44710 of Banbury shed waits there to take over the 8.30am Newcastle (Central) to Poole train on 24 June 1966. The train, seen on the left, had arrived behind Brush Type 4 diesel-electric No D1773 (later No 47178, then 47588).

Below right: No D1773 now heads the northbound 10.30am Poole to Newcastle (Central) train. Bulleid rebuilt 'West Country' 'Pacific' No 34012 *Launceston*, but lacking both name and number plates, which had brought the train in from Poole, can be seen taking water in the bay platform. The last point before arrival at Banbury where the engine could have taken water was Basingstoke. BR(WR) refused to provide any steam facilities at Oxford.

Part 8: BATH (Green Park), TEMPLECOMBE and HIGHBRIDGE

Train services

Bath (Green Park) to Bristol and the North

Many of my memories of the trains using Bath (Green Park) station and shed are described in my *Bath Recollections* book. I have therefore covered them briefly here and have extended my 'recollections' from Bath westwards to Bristol and south to Templecombe and Highbridge.

The emphasis placed by many railway publications on the trains using Bath (Green Park) station on summer Saturdays has meant that the year-round services have been somewhat neglected. In the summer of 1965, three years after the through trains ended and the last year before closure, seven trains left Green Park for Bristol (Temple Meads) each weekday, with an additional train at 12.25pm on Saturdays. Three of these had come from Bournemouth West. The trains offered an alternative way of getting to Bristol, although taking much longer to do so. The price of a ticket was the same and the service had the advantage of passing Bristol (Barrow Hill) shed where engines might be spotted.

My favourite train was the 10.10am from Green Park, which connected with the 10.30am from Bristol (Temple Meads) to Newcastle at Mangotsfield, which I caught several times to reach Gloucester (Eastgate) or Birmingham (New Street). In the early 1960s the Bath train would be hauled by an Ivatt Class 2 2-6-2 tank, but after 1962 Standard

Bath (Green Park) and Bitton

Right: BR Standard Class 3 2-6-2 tank No 82041 stands in Bath (Green Park) station with the 10.10am train for Bristol (Temple Meads) on 9 September 1965. I had used this train frequently to travel to Bristol, but this would be my last time. From January 1966 'Hymeks' took over the two remaining daily workings.

Below right: Standard Class 3 2-6-2 tanks continued to be used on these trains on Saturdays until the end of December. Here No 82044 is seen from the closed goods yard as it leaves Bitton with the 11.40am train from Bournemouth (Central) to Bristol (Temple Meads) on 6 November 1965. After the closure of Bournemouth (West) that October, trains to Bath (Green Park) used the Central station instead. As a result some interesting through carriage workings were introduced; in this case the coaches had started their day as part of a train from Waterloo to Bournemouth.

Class 3 tanks dominated the service. Despite the use of 'Peak' Class diesel-electrics on fill-in turns from Bristol (Bath Road) diesel depot, these became the last regularly steam-hauled trains to reach Bristol. They disappeared from Monday 3 January 1966 when BR(WR) introduced its 'Revised Service' from Bath (Green Park). After this just two 'Hymek'-worked trains ran daily between the two cities until Green Park station closed from 7 March.

Until September 1962 the 'Pines Express', of course, ran daily between Bournemouth and Sheffield (Midland), Liverpool (Lime Street) and Manchester (Piccadilly) throughout the year. The train was almost always hauled by a 'Black 5' but, between the summers of 1960 and the 1962, more interesting engines started to appear regularly. These included 'Jubilees', rebuilt 'Patriots', 'Royal Scots', and, as mentioned in Chapter 3, ex-LNER Class 'B1' 4-6-0s. These engines also appeared on the many inter-regional trains that ran via Green Park on summer Saturdays until September 1962. 'Peak' Class diesel-electrics took over the 'Pines Express' north of Bath from September 1961, although the last northbound train on 8 September was headed by 'Black 5' No 44659 as pictured on page 46.

In the same period goods traffic was steadily run down until by 1965 only coal traffic from Radstock to the power station at Portishead remained. For a time these trains were worked by Class '94XX' pannier tanks between Bath and Portishead.

Bath (Green Park) to Templecombe

During the winter the 'Pines Express' from Manchester (Piccadilly)/Liverpool (Lime Street) and Sheffield (Midland) to Bournemouth (West) was invariably headed out of Bath (Green Park) by a Standard Class 5 4-6-0 with an ex-LMS 2P 4-4-0 as pilot. Here 2P No 40634 heads the classic combination as the two engines climb out of Bath past Ringwood Road with the train in the late 1950s. The 2P, which would be removed at Evercreech Junction, was built for the S&D (No 45), to an LMS design, in 1928 and withdrawn in May 1962. The Standard Class 5 is almost certainly one of the three allocated to the line new in 1954, Nos 73050 to 73052. *Denis Horton*

One of the first six 7F 2-8-0s, No 53801, built at Derby in 1914, starts the descent of Devonshire Bank toward Bath with a coal train from Radstock in August 1961. The first of the Derby-built engines, No 53800 was withdrawn in July 1959, while No 53801 lasted until July 1961. *M. E. J. Deane collection, courtesy of Ian Bennett*

Right: The 3.20pm from Green Park to Templecombe had once provided a connection for intermediate stations for passengers off the southbound 'Pines Express', and continued to run after the express was diverted away from the S&D. By 1965 it was often in the hands of a BR Standard Class 4 2-6-4 tank, one of which, No 80059, is seen crossing Tucking Mill Viaduct with the train on 29 May 1965. The engine arrived at Templecombe in September 1964, moving to Green Park in July 1965. Its earlier sheds had included Neasden, Ashford (Kent) and Exmouth Junction. The engine was withdrawn that November.

Below: In 1951 BR(SR) transferred four 'West Country' 'Pacifics', Nos 34040/41/42 and 43, to Bath (Green Park). They were not particularly successful on the steep gradients on the line, but remained frequent visitors on summer Saturdays or Bank Holidays. The 'Pines Express' was then run as two trains, one of which did not require piloting out of Bath. Here No 34043 *Combe Martin* of Bournemouth shed (71B) gains the double track at the south end of Midford Viaduct with one of these trains in the early 1960s.
M. E. J. Deane collection, courtesy of Ian Bennett

Right: After the successful trial of a Stanier 8F 2-8-0 over the line in May 1961, the class started to replace the ex-S&D 7Fs. Here, during the summer of 1963, one of them crosses Midford Viaduct with a coal train from Radstock to the new power station at Portishead. The photograph was taken from the trackbed of the former Camerton to Limpley Stoke branch, which, having lost its passenger service in 1925, closed completely in 1951; as is well known, it was later used for the filming of *The Titfield Thunderbolt*.

Below: Radstock had its own engine shed, a sub-shed of Bath (Green Park), with an allocation of several 'Jinty' 0-6-0 tanks. In addition to their work around the various collieries, they were used to bank the heavy goods trains to Masbury summit. One of them, No 47496, is seen shunting in Norton Colliery near Midsomer Norton. Coal wagons were hauled in or out of the colliery by one of its own tank engines, including *Lord Salisbury*, an 0-6-0 saddle tank. No 47496 was withdrawn in November 1963. *M. E. J. Deane collection, courtesy of Ian Bennett*

Bath (Green Park) to Templecombe

As several of my grandmother's sisters lived around Bournemouth, my journeys over the ex-S&D line were fairly frequent. It is memorable that if we returned from Bournemouth (West) on the last train to Bath at 6.48pm, we would spend 39 minutes at Templecombe, eventually crawling into Bath at 10.12pm. The S&D might have been attractive to enthusiasts, but passengers on its trains had to be fairly resilient!

I made two journeys to Bournemouth West on the 'Pines Express' before it was diverted away from the line. The first was at Easter 1962 when, on Thursday 19 April, I travelled there with my aunt and grandmother. At Bank Holiday times the 'Pines' ran as two trains, from Manchester and Liverpool. We travelled on the latter train behind rebuilt 'West Country' 'Pacific' No 34046 *Braunton*, now preserved on the West Somerset Railway. I did not record what brought the train into Bath, but I did spot ex-MR 0-6-0 No 43682 as we passed Templecombe shed. The engine was one of the last of its class to be withdrawn, in September of that year, together with the last one built for the S&D, No 72, BR No 43216. On Saturday 8 September I again travelled to Bournemouth (West) on the 'Pines'. This time the train was hauled unaided by Standard 9F 2-10-0 No 92220 *Evening Star* on the train's last ever run via Bath (Green Park). With waving crowds all the way to Bournemouth it was a sad but memorable journey!

During 1964 I used the line several times to reach other steam-hauled services in the Bournemouth area. On 6 March I caught the 9.53am from Green Park, hauled by Standard Class 5 4-6-0 No 73049 to travel to Broadstone. On leaving Radstock (North) my train crossed the ex-GWR line from Radstock (West) to Bristol. By then the line was goods only and just after we'd crossed it 'Large Prairie' No 4101 appeared on a local goods from Bristol.

After climbing over the Mendips my train eventually ran into Templecombe. Here it connected with the 9.00am from Waterloo to Plymouth and Barnstaple Junction, which arrived behind 'Merchant Navy' 'Pacific' No 35023 *Holland-Afrika Line*. Ivatt Class 2 tank No 41243 then hauled our train out of the station, passing above Templecombe shed for the second time. Leaving No 41243 in our wake, my train headed south, passing the shed yet again. An account of my search for steam around Bournemouth is given in my book *The Last Years of BR Steam in Wessex: Southern Region*.

Between Radstock and Bath the coal traffic to the power station at Portishead was worked by Stanier 8F 2-8-0s. These engines had steadily replaced Fowler's S&D 7F 2-8-0s at Green Park shed from 1961.

Bath (Green Park) shed (82F, formerly BR(LMR) 22C and BR(SR) 71G): closed March 1966

82F

A view of the shed yard could be gained from this vantage point, reached through a door that stated 'Trespassers will be Prosecuted'. A prominent feature was the water-softening tower. The tank engine shunting the goods yard passed close by where we were standing; no doubt that was why one of the yard inspectors would rapidly expel us with veiled threats of prosecution, although the other was more understanding! Two former Midland Railway tenders used to take away the sludge are in the foreground, the second of which is still lettered 'LMS'. Next to them during the summer of 1961 is one of the 11 7F 2-8-0s built for the S&D, No 53806. The engine was the first of the five built by Robert Stephenson in Newcastle in 1925, and was withdrawn in January 1964.

Right: By 1960 the yard shunter at Bath (Green Park) was often ex-GWR pannier tank No 3742. Ex-LMS 'Jinty' 0-6-0 tanks also still made regular appearances, and one of the last to arrive at Bath, from Gloucester (Barnwood) shed, was No 47506. The engine is seen resting in the ex-Midland Railway shed at Bath on 27 October 1965. It was not withdrawn until March 1966. *John Price*

82G

Templecombe shed (83G, formerly BR(WR) 82G, BR(LMR) 22D and BR(SR) 71H): closed March 1966

Until 1960 the engines at Templecombe shed were of S&D, Midland or LMS origin, including 2P 4-4-0s and 3F and 4F 0-6-0s. Although not shedded there, at least one of the S&D's 7F 2-8-0s was also likely to be present. Several of the 2Ps were kept to pilot the heavy summer trains over the Mendip Hills and were stored during the winter. The scene during this period is well illustrated in the photo below. After this BR Standard Class 4 and 5 4-6-0s, Ivatt 2-6-2 tanks together with ex-GWR Class '2251' and Class '57XX' pannier tank 0-6-0s steadily replaced the older engines. Three ex-GWR Class '2251' 0-6-0s, Nos 2251, 3210 and 3216, were on shed as my train passed by on 20 March 1964.

When I visited the shed on 10 July 1965 I noted 14 engines. Eight of these were Ivatt tanks, three were Standard Class 4 tanks, engines that first appeared on the line in September 1964, and two were ex-GWR pannier tanks. Also present was Standard Class 5 4-6-0 No 73054 of Bath (Green Park) shed. My last visit was on Friday 4 March 1966 when the only engine in steam was the shed pilot, Ivatt tank No 41283. The shed closed from Monday 7 March.

Above: After 1961 Green Park shed received a steady stream of Stanier 2-8-0s, which replaced the ex-S&D 7Fs, until the Stanier engines were themselves withdrawn. One of the class to arrive in the summer of 1965 was No 48444. The Swindon-built engine is seen waiting to be turned at Green Park shed on 27 October 1965. It was withdrawn in February 1966. *John Price*

Templecombe shed (82G, then 83G, ex-LMS 22D, BR(SR) 71H)

Left: Ex-Midland/LMS engines are still well in evidence at Templecombe shed in August 1960. Nearest to the camera is 2P 4-4-0 No 40537 followed, after the mineral wagon, by 2P No 40569. Beyond again is an Ivatt Class 2 2-6-2 tank, another 2P, a Stanier Class 3 2-6-2 tank and a 'Jinty' tank, with an unidentified engine at the front. Behind the shed building are 2P No 40564, a 3F 0-6-0 and a larger engine, possibly an ex-S&D 7F. Most of the 2Ps would have been active the previous Saturday piloting holiday trains over the Mendip Hills, work they continued to do until the end of the summer of 1961. Although subsequently rebuilt, No 40537 dated from 1899 and was the last of its class to be withdrawn, in September 1962.
M. E. J. Deane collection, courtesy of Ian Bennett

Train services

Evercreech Junction to Highbridge for Burnham-on-Sea

At Evercreech Junction trains between Bath and Templecombe connected with those on the branch to Highbridge for Burnham-on-Sea. The station at Burnham-on-Sea had closed in October 1951, but continued to be used by the occasional summer excursion until September 1962. In 1964 goods traffic was still handled at Highbridge Wharf (although not from the sea!), which meant that trains still crossed the Bristol to Taunton main line on the level. The last station before reaching Highbridge was Bason Bridge, from where milk tankers had once travelled to London via Templecombe; since the BR(WR) take-over these now travelled via Highbridge and also used the crossing to reach the main line.

I made four journeys from Highbridge to Evercreech Junction, each behind a different class of engine: ex-LMS 0-6-0 No 44417 on 8 March 1963, ex-GWR Class '2251' No 2217 0-6-0 on 18 September 1964, pannier tank No 3659 on 8 September 1965, and finally Ivatt Class 2 tank No 41249 on Saturday 5 March 1966. Although the Ivatt tanks had first appeared at Highbridge to replace ex-S&D/MR 0-4-4 tanks in 1959, it was not until the very last train on the very last day of public passenger services that I travelled behind one.

Right: Five years later, on 10 July 1965, ex-GWR pannier, Ivatt Class 2 2-6-2 and BR Standard Class 4 2-6-4 tanks dominate the scene at Templecombe shed. The engines present are Nos 4631, 9647, 41243 and 80067 had just been withdrawn. The other engines survived into 1966.

Centre right: Ivatt Class 2 2-6-2 No 41283 is the shed pilot at Templecombe on 4 March 1966, just two days before closure.

Evercreech Junction to Highbridge for Burnham-on-Sea

Below: Ex-GWR Class '2251' 0-6-0 No 2218 is seen at Glastonbury & Street station in the summer of 1964. During this period several '2251s'were based at Templecombe for use on these trains. The engine was withdrawn in November 1964. *M. E. J. Deane collection, courtesy of Ian Bennett*

Above: The Highbridge branch was a last retreat for several ex-Midland Railway engines, including 3F 0-6-0s. One of these, No 43593, seen leaving Highbridge during August 1959, was not withdrawn until November 1960. No 43216, built for the S&D (No 72) by Neilson & Co in 1902, lasted until September 1962, when it was withdrawn from Templecombe shed. *M. E. J. Deane collection, courtesy of Ian Bennett*

Above right: Another S&D-based Class '2251', No 3201, crosses the BR(WR) main line at Highbridge with milk tankers from Bason Bridge on 18 September 1964. This milk traffic had formerly run to Templecombe for its onward journey to London. No 3203 survived until May 1965.

Right: The last time I travelled on the branch was on 5 March 1966 when I caught the 4.00pm from Highbridge to Evercreech Junction. This was also the last scheduled train on the branch. Here Ivatt Class 2 2-6-2 tank No 41249 drops down from Highbridge shed to join its train. After taking water at Evercreech Junction the train and its many passengers proceeded unscheduled to Templecombe.

Highbridge shed (BR (LMR) 22E, BR(SR) 71J, then sub-shed to Templecombe): closed March 1966

I visited the small four-road engine shed once on Sunday 26 May 1963. Here I found Class '2251' 0-6-0 No 3210 and Ivatt Class 2 2-6-2 tank No 41296.

The last days of public services on the S&D: 6/7 March 1966

The 'Revised Service' between Bath and Bournemouth and between Evercreech Junction and Highbridge, introduced on Monday 3 January 1966, provided just four trains each way over the S&D line. Trains from Bath ran only as far as Templecombe, calling at all stations. The only through train to Bath (Green Park) left Bournemouth (Central) at 6.45pm and arrived at 9.50pm. Just two trains ran daily in each direction over the Highbridge branch.

The only southbound train, which required piloting out of Templecombe's Upper station, was the 4.13pm from Evercreech Junction to Bournemouth Central. On Friday 4 March I travelled by motor scooter to Templecombe to photograph this manoeuvre for the last time. The train, which had earlier left Templecombe as the 3.30pm to Evercreech Junction behind BR Standard Class 4 2-6-0 No 76005, returned and ran up into the station. Ivatt tank No 41290 followed it into the station and a few minutes later drew the train out again. I last saw it passing the small and little-used platform of Templecombe Lower.

Next day I travelled from Highbridge on the very last departure, the 4.00pm to Evercreech Junction, which was hauled by Ivatt tank No 41249. Although not advertised to do so, the train

Left: The engine shed at Highbridge is seen in this view of 26 May 1963. On shed at the time were Ivatt 2-6-2 tank No 41206 and 0-6-0 No 3210. The buildings of the S&D's Highbridge Works are just visible behind the shed.

The last few days of the S&D: March 1966

In the emergency timetable for the ex-S&D line introduced on Monday 3 January 1966 were just four trains between Templecombe and Bath (Green Park), and only one of these was a through train, which left Bournemouth (Central) at 6.46pm. Here the 2.00pm from Templecombe is seen near Masbury summit on 4 March 1966 hauled by BR Standard Class 4 2-6-4 tank No 80041. The next day, Saturday 5 March, the engine was to bring the last service train into Bath (Green Park), double-headed with sister engine No 80043.

Above: Bournemouth-based Standard Class 4 2-6-0 No 76005 arrives at Templecombe with the 4.13pm from Evercreech Junction to Bournemouth (Central) on 4 March 1966. This was the only southbound train in the emergency timetable not to terminate at Templecombe.

continued from Evercreech Junction to Templecombe. There I waited, together with many others, to catch the last train to Bath (Green Park), the 6.45pm from Bournemouth (Central). The train, double-headed by two Standard Class 4 2-6-4 tanks, Nos 80041 and 80043, was eventually hauled up into the station by an Ivatt tank. It was a memorable journey as, despite the darkness at each station, many people waited to say their farewells to the S&D, while approaching Bath there was a cacophony of sound as detonators exploded..

Two special trains ran over the S&D on the Sunday. The last departure from Bath (Green Park) was an RCTS special headed by rebuilt 'West Country' 'Pacific' No 34013 *Okehampton* and unrebuilt 'Battle of Britain' 'Pacific' No 34057 *Biggin Hill*. The train had earlier traversed the Highbridge branch behind Ivatt tanks Nos 41283 and 41249. The very last arrival at Bath (Green Park) was an SLS special, which had left Bath that morning for Bournemouth, headed by two Green Park engines, 8F 2-8-0 No 48706 and Standard Class 4 tank No 80043. The line had thwarted BR's plan to eliminate steam at the end of December 1965 by just over two months.

Above: Ivatt tank No 41290 hauls the 4.13pm from Evercreech Junction to Bournemouth (Central) out of Templecombe Upper station on 4 March 1966. No 76005 is on the rear of the train.

Above left: With No 76005 once more at its head, the 4.13pm from Evercreech Junction to Bournemouth (Central) passes the single, little-used Templecombe Lower platform on the same day.

Sunday 6 March 1966 was the final day, and saw two special trains depart from Bath (Green Park). The first was the SLS special from Green Park to Bournemouth (Central) and return. The train is seen here at Templecombe hauled by ex-LMS Stanier 8F 2-8-0 No 48706 and Standard Class 4 2-6-4 tank No 80043. On its return the train became the last ever arrival at Bath (Green Park). *M. E. J. Deane collection, courtesy of Ian Bennett*

The second special on Sunday 6 March was organised by the RCTS. It arrived at Bath (Green Park) from Highbridge via Bristol (Temple Meads) and, in the early evening, left again behind rebuilt 'West Country' 'Pacific' No 34013 *Okehampton* and unrebuilt 'Battle of Britain' 'Pacific' No 34057 *Biggin Hill*. It was the last passenger train ever to climb Devonshire Bank out of Bath and over the Mendips to Templecombe. It passed the returning SLS special en route.

Permits issued to the author to visit engine sheds in Bristol, Westbury, Yeovil and Taunton

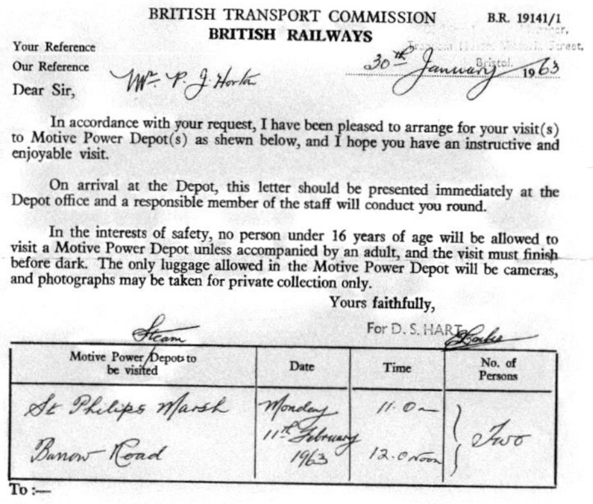

BRITISH TRANSPORT COMMISSION B.R. 19141/1
BRITISH RAILWAYS

Bristol.

Your Reference
Our Reference
Mr. P. J. Horton 30th January 1963
Dear Sir,

In accordance with your request, I have been pleased to arrange for your visit(s) to Motive Power Depot(s) as shewn below, and I hope you have an instructive and enjoyable visit.

On arrival at the Depot, this letter should be presented immediately at the Depot office and a responsible member of the staff will conduct you round.

In the interests of safety, no person under 16 years of age will be allowed to visit a Motive Power Depot unless accompanied by an adult, and the visit must finish before dark. The only luggage allowed in the Motive Power Depot will be cameras, and photographs may be taken for private collection only.

Yours faithfully,

Steam

For D. S. HART

Motive Power Depots to be visited	Date	Time	No. of Persons
St Philips Marsh	Monday 11th February 1963	11.0	Two
Barrow Road		12.0 Noon	

To :—

Permit for Bristol sheds, 11 February 1963.

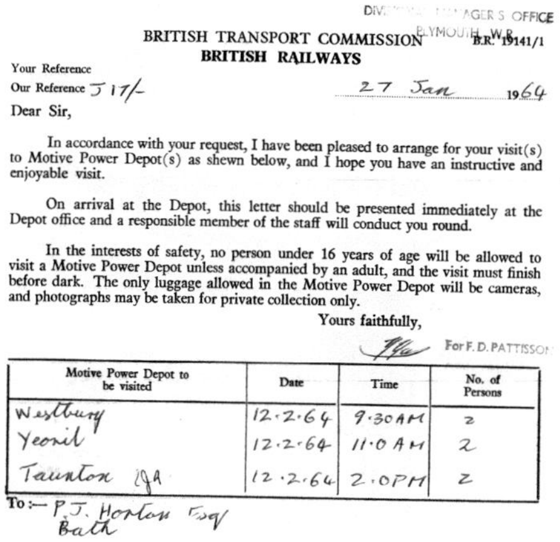

DIV... ...AGER'S OFFICE
PLYMOUTH W.R.

BRITISH TRANSPORT COMMISSION B.R. 19141/1
BRITISH RAILWAYS

Your Reference
Our Reference J 17/-
27 Jan 1964
Dear Sir,

In accordance with your request, I have been pleased to arrange for your visit(s) to Motive Power Depot(s) as shewn below, and I hope you have an instructive and enjoyable visit.

On arrival at the Depot, this letter should be presented immediately at the Depot office and a responsible member of the staff will conduct you round.

In the interests of safety, no person under 16 years of age will be allowed to visit a Motive Power Depot unless accompanied by an adult, and the visit must finish before dark. The only luggage allowed in the Motive Power Depot will be cameras, and photographs may be taken for private collection only.

Yours faithfully,

For F. D. PATTISSON

Motive Power Depot to be visited	Date	Time	No. of Persons
Westbury	12.2.64	9.30 AM	2
Yeovil	12.2.64	11.0 AM	2
Taunton 2JA	12.2.64	2.0 PM	2

To :— P.J. Horton Esq
Bath

Permit for Westbury, Yeovil and Taunton, 12 February 64.

Index to locations